IMAGES OF WAR

FIGHTERS UNDER CONSTRUCTION IN WORLD WAR TWO

RARE PHOTOGRAPHS FROM WARTIME ARCHIVES

GRAHAM M. SIMONS

Pen & Sword
AVIATION

First published in Great Britain in 2013 by
PEN & SWORD AVIATION
an imprint of
Pen & Sword Books Ltd,
47 Church Street,
Barnsley,
South Yorkshire.
S70 2AS

Copyright © Graham M Simons, 2013

A CIP catalogue record for this book is available from the British Library

ISBN 978 1 78159 034 8

The right of Graham M Simons to be identified as Author of
this Work has been asserted by them in accordance with the
Copyright, Designs and Patents Act 1988.

Printed and bound in England
By CPI Group (UK) Ltd, Croydon, CR0 4YY

Pen & Sword Books Ltd incorporates the imprints of Pen & Sword Aviation,
Pen & Sword Family History, Pen & Sword Maritime, Pen & Sword Military,
Pen & Sword Discovery, Wharncliffe Local History Wharncliffe True Crime,
Wharncliffe Transport, Pen & Sword Select, Sword Military Classics,
Leo Cooper, The Praetorian Press, Remember When,
Seaforth Publishing and Frontline Publishing.

For a complete list of Pen & Sword titles please contact:
Pen & Swords Books Limited

47 Church Street, Barnsley, South Yorkshire, S70 2AS, England.
E-mail: enquiries@pen-and-sword.co.uk
Website: www.pen-and-sword.co.uk

CONTENTS

SELECTED TECHNICAL GLOSSARY

Alclad	the trademark of Alcoa used as a generic term to describe corrosion resistant aluminium sheet formed from high-purity aluminium surface layers metallurgically bonded to high strength aluminium alloy core material.
Broaching	a machining process that uses a toothed tool, called a broach, to remove material.
Burr	a sharp edge created after machining.
Bush	a metal collar; can be a bearing or also a hardened guide for a cutting tool.
Bush plate	a device to hold a series of bushes for multiple hole drilling etc.
Butt-strap	a strap or plate covering a butt joint and secured to both pieces.
Die	a specialized tool used in manufacturing industries to cut or shape material using a press
Dimpling	a slight depression in a surface; often used to give strength to a flat sheet.
Duralumin	the trade name of one of the earliest types of age-hardenable aluminium alloys.
Finish ream	to use a reamer, which is a metalworking tool used to create an accurate sized hole.
Fixture	a device that holds the item to be worked on.
Former	a previously manufactured 'shape' around which metal can be bent.
Gauge	a device used to determine the exact dimensions of an item; a measurement (often stated as a number) of how large a wire or metal sheet is, either in diameter or cross sectional area.
Indexing	an operation of dividing a periphery of a cylindrical workpiece into equal number of divisions by the help of index crank and index plate.
Jig	a device to guide the tool towards the item to be worked on, but does not hold the item to be machined.
Joggle	a joint between two pieces of material formed by a notch and a fitted projection.
Lapping	a machining operation, in which two surfaces are rubbed together with an abrasive between them, by hand movement or by way of a machine.
Layshaft	a secondary shaft, as in a sliding change gear; a camshaft operated by a two-to-one gear in an internal-combustion engine.
Longeron	a thin strip of wood or metal to which the skin of the aircraft is fastened.
Moncocque	a construction technique that supports structural load by using an object's external skin.
Nitriding	a heat treating process that diffuses nitrogen into the surface of a metal to create a hardened surface to a specific depth.
Panting	the movement of a metal sheet in a manner similar to a person breathing.
Poppet valve	used to control the timing and quantity of gas or vapour flow into an engine. It consists of a hole, usually round or oval, and a tapered plug, usually a disk shape on the end of a shaft also called a valve stem. Trunnion a cylindrical protrusion used as a mounting and/or pivoting point.
Scarfing	a method of joining two members end to end in woodworking or metalworking.
Sleeve valve	a valve that fits between the piston and the cylinder wall in the cylinder of an engine where it rotates and/or slides, aligning with the cylinder's inlet and exhaust ports at the appropriate stages in the engine's cycle.
Spindling	to use a woodworking tool to cut receses in otder to 'add lightness'
Stringer	a strip of wood or metal to which the skin of an aircraft is fastened

They Who Also Serve...

There has been bookshelf after bookshelf of books compiled, written and published about British aircraft, the Royal Air Force and the activities of its pilots during World War Two. Tales of derring do, bravery and gallantry quite rightly litter the bookshelves and libraries, but little has appeared in print about the what could be called the unsung heroes, those that designed, built and maintained the fighting equipment used to eventually defeat the enemy.

This is all the more incredible when one realises that there exists a huge archive of images that have survived which clearly show the skills and scale of what went on. These images of war - many of which are seen here for almost the first time in seventy years - form a remarkable tribute to the designers, engineers and workers who did so much.

A series of Expansions...

Following the end of the Great War, the Royal Air Force was drastically reduced in both manpower and equipment. The application of a 'Ten Year Rule' in which the British Government foresaw no war being fought during the next ten years resulted in minimal defence expenditure throughout the 1920s. These budgetary constraints resulted in many squadrons having to struggle on through the same period with aircraft originally designed during World War One, such as the DH9A and Bristol F2B Fighter.

Each year the 'Ten Year Rule' was extended until the early 1930s, when it at last became apparent that Germany was developing expansionist and aggressive tendencies that could no longer be ignored. The British Government and Air Ministry at last began to develop plans of their own to expand and develop the Royal Air Force. A number of plans were approved by the Cabinet, but each one was often replaced by a revised one before the original could be completed.

Between 1933 and 1939 the Royal Air Force was given higher priority in terms of rearmament plans than the other services. The policy was driven by the pursuit of parity with Germany more than by defence and strike needs, for there was no fixed ratio of bombers to fighter aircraft to guide procurement.

Of all the RAF expansion schemes between 1934 and 1939, only scheme F was actually completed. Importantly, this scheme included realistic numbers of reserve aircraft and personnel, something that the earlier schemes had failed to do. The RAF also issued requirements for modern fighters in 1935, and heavy bombers in 1936. In November 1938 the emphasis moved from bombers to fighter defence, but delays meant that modern aircraft were in short supply. To demonstrate how things changed: in 1934 42 squadrons existed, providing a first line strength of some 800 aircraft. By 1939 this had grown four-fold. At the same time there had been a major increase in aircraft and aero-engine production and a rapid expansion of training to provide the new air and ground crews.

As a result of this expansion there was naturally a severe shortage of manufacturing facilities. Existing aircraft manufacturers did not have ability to cope, so a plan was developed by the British Government to implement additional manufacturing capacity for the British aircraft industry. Developed by the Air Ministry under the internal project name of the Shadow Scheme, the project was created by Sir Kingsley Wood, the Secretary of State for Air, and headed by Herbert Austin.

The Shadow Scheme saw many locations around the country handed over to companies for the purpose of aircraft or aero-engine production and is worthy of a book in itself. As the war progressed, it seemed that the whole of the country was involved in aircraft parts manufacture.

In general terms, each outside contractor was responsible for certain components, and concentrated and specialised on only one or two portions of the aircraft. For this outside production, special arrangements had to be made to deal with imparting the necessary information to the firms concerned.

Usually a special department was formed at the parent company, known as the Outside Production Office, to deal with the expansion of production of whatever aircraft it was, in addition to extensive repairs to existing aircraft. Staff was also sent out from the works to help the daughter firms in their production.

The functions of the Outside Production Office were briefly as follows:—
    (a) To arrange facilities at the parent firm's works for key workers to receive training in production methods and inspection.
    (b) To supply technical information, including supplies of copies of drawings, modifications and planning sheets.
    (c) To arrange for the supply of templates, sample parts and components for use in the preparation of jigs and tools.
    (d) To supply information and drawings for all tooling equipment.
    (e) To assist daughter firms in the selection of tools and equipment.
    (f) To answer all queries raised by and through daughter firms in connection with methods of manufacture.
    (g) To render advice and give technical approval on repairs and also approve where possible parts which were not to drawing and might otherwise be scrapped.

Production was divided between two main groups. The parent firm had a local sub-office to deal with all technical queries arising from shop errors and rectifications, etc., which acted in a decentralized capacity to give technical decisions which if referred to head office might only be obtained with considerable delay.

All firms concerned in the Production Group had considerable administrative and manufacturing experience and were fully competent to deal completely with matters arising out of their contracts as between themselves and the Ministry of Aircraft Production. From a contractual point of view they were of equal status with the parent firm. Generally speaking, it was discovered that it was best to let each member of the Production Group arrange for its own sub-contracting.

When it came to design changes, those of a major character were made to meet differing conditions in the field. These and other changes were discussed at a meeting of the principals from the Production Group firms under the chairmanship of the Director-General of Aircraft Production. Any changes necessary to give improvement in performance or to meet the changing conditions in service were viewed every fortnight by the Local Technical Committee at the parent firm's works. This committee was made up of senior representatives from the parent firm's technical and production staff and also from the Air Ministry. The daughter firms provided representatives present at these meetings to keep them up to date with new developments and to give their views on production matters.

SPITFIRE!

Original Caption: Supermarine Spitfire I eight-gun single-seater fighters, believed to be the fastest military aircraft in large-scale production in the world, on the final assembly line at Southampton. Rolls-Royce Merlin IIs are awaiting installation in the foreground. Despite its extreme performance the Spitfire is reasonably easy to build and even easier to fly.

The Supermarine Spitfire was a British single-seat fighter aircraft used by the Royal Air Force and many other Allied countries throughout the Second World War. It continued to be used into the 1950s both as a front line fighter and in secondary roles. It was produced in greater numbers than any other British aircraft and was the only Allied fighter in production throughout the war.

The Spitfire was designed as a short-range high-performance interceptor machine by R. J. Mitchell, chief designer at Supermarine Aviation Works (from 1928 a subsidiary of Vickers-Armstrong). Mitchell continued to refine the design until his death from cancer in 1937, whereupon his colleague Joseph Smith became chief designer. The Spitfire's elliptical wing had a thin cross-section, allowing a higher top speed than several contemporary fighters. Speed was seen as essential to carry out the mission of home defence against enemy bombers.

Above: a line of assembly fixtures for the monocoque main section of the fuselage.

Mitchell's design aims were to create a well-balanced, high-performance bomber interceptor and fighter aircraft capable of fully exploiting the power of the Merlin engine, while being relatively easy to fly.

From the seventh frame, to which the pilot's seat and (later) armour plating was attached, to the nineteenth, which was mounted at a slight forward angle just forward of the fin, the frames were oval, each reducing slightly in size and each with numerous holes drilled through them to lighten them as much as possible without weakening them.

Right: A close up of one of the main fuselage assembly fixtures in which the assembly and plating of the monocoque portion was completed.

The Spitfire's airframe was complex: the streamlined, semi-monocoque duralumin fuselage featured a large number of compound curves built up from a skeleton of frames, starting from the main engine bulkhead to the tail unit attachment frame. Aft of the engine bulkhead were five half-frames to accommodate the fuel tanks and cockpit.

Once the frames were skinned the fuselage was transferred to a series of jigs for a number of machining processes.

These jigs formed a guide for the tools used in a machining operation.

Left: the jig in which the attachment holes in the stub spars were finish-reamed and the wing-root fillet attachment holes drilled.

Paired-up assembly fixtures for rear fuselage units.

The U-shaped frame 20 was the last frame of the fuselage proper and the frame to which the tail unit was attached. Frames 21, 22 and 23 formed the fin; frame 22 incorporated the tailwheel opening and frame 23 was the rudder post. Before being attached to the main fuselage, the tail unit frames were held in a jig and the eight horizontal tail formers were riveted to them.

A combination of fourteen longitudinal stringers and two main longerons helped form a light but rigid structure to which sheets of alclad stressed skinning were attached. The fuselage plating was 24, 20 and 18 gauge thickness in order of thickness towards the tail, while the fin structure was completed using short longerons from frames 20 to 23, before being covered in 22 gauge plating.

Right: Spitfire Mk IIA, P7666, EB-Z, 'Observer Corps', was built by Castle Bromwich, and delivered to 41 Squadron on 23 November 1940.

Left: first stage showing the structural framework almost completed.

Mitchell has sometimes been accused of copying the wing shape of the Heinkel He 70, which first flew in 1932; but as Beverly Shenstone, the aerodynamicist on Mitchell's team, explained 'Our wing was much thinner and had quite a different section to that of the Heinkel. In any case it would have been simply asking for trouble to have copied a wing shape from an aircraft designed for an entirely different purpose.

Below: a port wing structure in the main assembly fixture. The skin plating has been applied to the upper surface. Final stages of wing assembly were performed out of the fixture with the wing held in a felt-lined cradle.

Opposite page: a completed wing - with an undercarriage leg and wheel - sits in a felt-lined cradle awaiting to be turned through ninety degrees and placed on a flat trolley (right) before being moved to the Spitfire final assembly line. The spar roots were mounted at the correct assembly height.

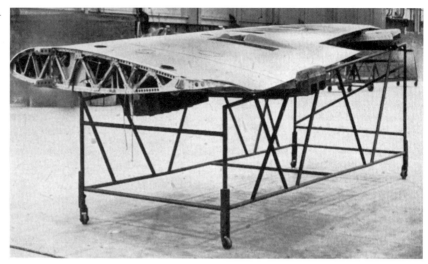

Below: Lowering the Rolls-Royce Merlin engine on to its mounting in the early stages of intermediate assembly.

The tubular engine mounting for the Spitfire was assembled in the inverted position.

The skins of the fuselage, wings and tailplane were secured by rivets and in critical areas such as the wing forward of the main spar where an uninterrupted airflow was required, with flush rivets; the fuselage used standard dome-headed riveting. From February 1943 flush riveting was used on the fuselage, affecting all Spitfire variants.

Right: twin fixtures for the assembly of the tailplane surface.

The wings, supported in cradles on wheeled trolleys at the correct height in readiness for bolting up to the fuselage.

A feature of the wing which contributed greatly to its success was the innovative spar boom design, made up of five square tubes which fitted into each other. As the wing thinned out along its span the tubes were progressively cut away in a similar fashion to a leaf spring; two of these booms were linked together by an alloy web, creating a lightweight and very strong main spar.

The undercarriage legs were attached to pivot points built into the inner, rear section of the main spar and retracted outwards and slightly backwards into wells in the non-load-carrying wing structure. The resultant narrow undercarriage track was considered to be an acceptable compromise as this reduced the bending loads on the main spar during landing.

Ahead of the spar, the thick-skinned leading edge of the wing formed a strong and rigid D-shaped box, which took most of the wing loads. The radiators were housed in a new radiator-duct designed by Fredrick Meredith of the RAE at Farnborough; this used the cooling air to generate thrust, greatly reducing the net drag produced by the radiators. The leading-edge structure was later adapted to house integral fuel tanks of various sizes.

The British public first saw the Spitfire at the RAF Hendon air-display on Saturday 27 June 1936. Although full-scale production was supposed to begin immediately, there were numerous problems which could not be overcome for some time and the first production Spitfire, K9787, did not roll off the Woolston, Southampton assembly line until mid-1938.

All of the main flight controls on the Spitfire were originally metal structures with fabric covering. Designers and pilots thought that having ailerons which were too heavy to move at high speed would avoid possible aileron reversal, stopping pilots throwing the aircraft around and pulling the wings off. It was also felt that air combat would take place at relatively low speed and that high-speed manoeuvring would be physically impossible.

However, during the Battle of Britain, pilots found the ailerons of the Spitfire were far too heavy at high speeds, severely restricting lateral manoeuvres such as rolls and high speed turns, which were still a feature of air-to-air combat. Flight tests showed the fabric covering of the ailerons 'ballooned' at high speeds, adversely affecting the aerodynamics. Replacing the fabric covering with light alloy dramatically improved the ailerons at high speed.

An undercarriage-actuation test being performed in the later stages of final assembly.

Original caption: Symbolic of Supermarine's success in the construction of marine aircraft, Stranraers and Walruses form a fitting background for this convincing array of Spitfire single-seater fighters in production. Powered by a Rolls-Royce Merlin engine and peerless among standard fighters in performance and manoeuvrability, the Spitfire is by no means the 'tricky' production job which might be imagined. Construction is all-metal with a monocoque fuselage.

The first and most immediate problem was that the main Supermarine factory at Woolston was already working at full capacity fulfilling orders for Walrus and Stranraer flying boats. Although outside contractors were supposed to be involved in manufacturing many important Spitfire components, especially the wings, Vickers-Armstrong (the parent company) were reluctant to see the Spitfire being manufactured by outside concerns and were slow to release the necessary blueprints and subcomponents. As a result of the delays in getting the Spitfire into full production, the Air Ministry put forward a plan that production of the Spitfire be stopped after the initial order for 310, after which Supermarine would build Bristol Beaufighters. The managements of Supermarine and Vickers were able to persuade the Air Ministry that the problems could be overcome and further orders were placed for 200 Spitfires on 24 March 1938, the two orders covering the K, L and N prefix serial numbers.

In 1935, the Air Ministry approached Morris Motor Company to ask how quickly their Cowley plant could be turned to aircraft production. This informal enquiry regarding major manufacturing facilities was turned into a formal plan to boost British aircraft production capacity in 1936, as the Shadow factory plan, under the leadership of Herbert Austin. Austin was briefed to build nine new factories, and further supplement the existing British car manufacturing industry, by either adding to its overall capacity or capability to reorganise to produce aircraft and their engines.

Under the terms of the Shadow Plan, on 12 July 1938, the Air Ministry bought a site consisting of farm fields and a sewage works next to Castle Bromwich airfield in Birmingham. This shadow factory would supplement Supermarine's original factories in Southampton in building the Spitfire. The Castle Bromwich Aircraft Factory ordered the most modern machine tools then available, which were being installed two months after work started on the site. Although Morris Motors under Lord Nuffield (an expert in mass motor-vehicle construction) at first managed and equipped the factory, it was funded by government money. When the project was first mooted it was estimated that the factory would be built for £2,000,000, however, by the beginning of 1939 this cost had doubled to over £4,000,000.

The Spitfire's stressed-skin construction required precision engineering skills and techniques outside the experience of the local labour force, which took some time to train. However, even as the first Spitfires were being built in June 1940, the factory was still incomplete and there were numerous problems with the factory management, which ignored tooling and drawings provided by Supermarine in favour of tools and drawings of its own designs. With the workforce, while not completely stopping production, continually threatened strikes or 'slow downs' until their demands for higher than average pay rates were met.

Here Spitfires come together, as the original caption describes: 'Lines of Spitfire fuselages in process of erection at a Government shadow factory. In contrast to that of its equally famous British counterpart, the Spitfire fuselage is of monocoque type with metal stressed skin covering. Plating operations are shown in progress on the centre line of fuselages, while a further row of camouflaged units may be seen on the right.

AN ORGANIC SPITFIRE?

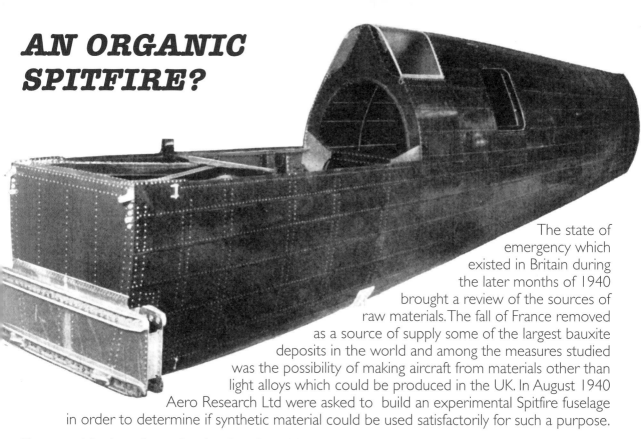

The state of emergency which existed in Britain during the later months of 1940 brought a review of the sources of raw materials. The fall of France removed as a source of supply some of the largest bauxite deposits in the world and among the measures studied was the possibility of making aircraft from materials other than light alloys which could be produced in the UK. In August 1940 Aero Research Ltd were asked to build an experimental Spitfire fuselage in order to determine if synthetic material could be used satisfactorily for such a purpose.

The material selected was Gordon Aerolite, which had been developed by the company as a result of research into the problem of producing a suitable synthetic material for moulded airscrew blades. Gordon Aerolite was made of untwisted fibres of flax impregnated with phenolic resin and made into bands approximately six inches in width on a machine developed for the purpose. To make sheet material a number of bands were placed edge to edge and overlaid by others placed at right angles to build up the required thickness. The pack of strips was then hot-pressed to bond them into a single sheet.

Tests on the material were made by the Royal Aircraft Establishment at Farnborough and as a result the opinion was expressed that Gordon Aerolite was then the most promising organic sheet material available as a possible stressed-skin covering for aircraft. It was considered probable that, if it could be made available in quantity, it might be used as a direct substitute to replace light-alloy sheet in existing designs. The material had approximately equal strength and stiffness along and across the sheet, but the strength and stiffness at 45 degrees to the grain was only one-half that along the fibres. As in plywood, the latter property could actually be an advantage where it was required to bend the material round a sharp curve.

In applying this material for airframe construction Aero Research used it on this basis as a direct substitute. Development of a specialized technique to take advantage of any particular property of the material was not attempted: time was an important factor and it was decided to adhere closely to existing assembly practice in order to avoid any break in production should a changeover to the new material become necessary. Gordon Aerolite sheet was used for all the structural members, including the frames, longerons and stringers and, in general, the design followed closely that of the original Spitfire. Except in the majority of the frames, which were built up on a flat, steam-heated plate with Ardux cement, riveting was used throughout in assembly.

As a preliminary to the construction of the complete fuselage, the rear section from frames 19 to 25 was made. It was tested at the Royal Aircraft Establishiment against the corresponding section of a metal Spitfire fuselage. As a result of these tests the complete Gordon Aerolite fuselage was stiffened in the region of the opening for batteries at the rear end.

As already stated, all structural parts of the fuselage were of Gordon Aerolite, but cellulose-acetate sheet and cotton-reinforced phenol-formaldehyde sheet were used in a few subsidiary portions where they offered advantages. At the top of the fuselage, the fairing between frames 18 and 19 was made of black cellulose-acetate sheet and the transparent acetate sheet secured with Plastel stainless steel to give a flush finish.

The fuselage in Gordon Aerolite was of the same total weight as the production fuselage in light alloy. The construction of this fuselage may be regarded as having been something in the nature of an extreme insurance policy to cover a fairly remote but nevertheless possible emergency. Although the need for this type of construction never actually arose, the experiment was justified by the circumstances and the results obtained. It affords an interesting example of what can be done with alternative materials and ,incidentally, a convincing demonstration of the determined spirit which informed the country at that time of crisis.

Left: part of the forward starboard side with the metal main spar members on Frame 5 to the left.

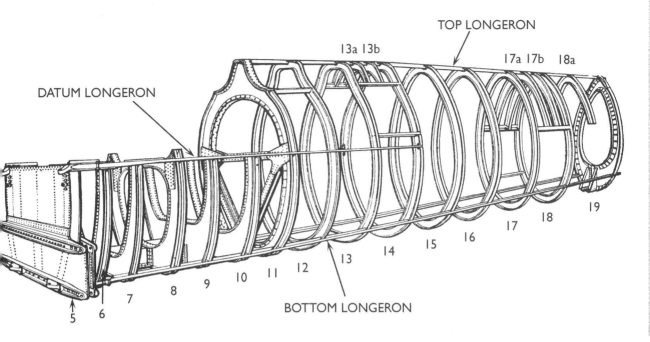

DATUM LONGERON

TOP LONGERON

13a 13b   17a 17b   18a

5 6 7 8 9 10 11 12 13 14 15 16 17 18 19

BOTTOM LONGERON

The Spitfire fuselage, from the forward main-spar frame (frame 5) to the joint with the tail section frame19) formed the subject of the experiment. The non-structural decking round the pilot's cockpit was omitted. Frames 12 to 19 were of single built-up channel section and frames 5 to 11 were heavier members made by riveting two single frames together. Spar members of the original material were embodied in frame 5.

Channel sections for the frames were composed of two L-section flanges of 0.6 inches by 0.5 inches by 0.6 inches. Gordon Aerolite joined by a flat web of the same material 0.05 inches in thickness. The web-attachment flange of each L-section was saw-cut at intervals to simplify bending to the contour of the fuselage section. Each frame was made in four sections, top, bottom and two sides that were butt-jointed together and reinforced by a strap of Gordon Aerolite 0.05 inches in thickness. Angles and webs were bonded on by Ardux glue on a steam-heated hotplate with pressure applied by hand cramps.

Right: bottom of the cockpit section showing frames 9 and 10 with the first complete frame 11 on the right.

The fixture on which the fuselage was assembled. Frame locations were mounted on an internal cantilever structure.

The skin covering consisted of planks or strakes of Gordon Aerolite sheet continuous over the entire length of the fuselage. Each strake decreased progressively in thickness from the forward to the after end. Between frames 5 and 8 the thickness was 0.11 inches and from frames 8 to 19 this thickness was gradually reduced to 0.045 inches. This varying section was obtained by building-up packs of Gordon Aerolite laminations, which were then bonded by being fed progressively through a 70-ton press. In order to obtain maximum torsional rigidity in the fuselage, the grain of the Gordon Aerolite sheet was inclined at an angle of 45 degrees to the edge of each strake.

The problem of obtaining the compound curves on the fuselage was solved in a similar manner to how plywood fuel-tanks were built. One edge of each strake was straight, but the other was cut to a curvature related to that required on the fuselage. By joining the straight edge of one strake to the adjacent curved edge of the next, a composite panel of compound curvature was obtained. A joggle was moulded along the straight edge of each strake to give a flush exterior surface at the lap joints between them. Countersunk rivets were used to keep everything together.

'A SPIT WIV AN 'OOK...' - THE SEAFIRE

That the Royal Navy, in urgent need of fighter aircraft with modern performance for fleet and convoy protection, should in the early years of the war have turned to the Hurricane and Spitfire for a solution of their problem was hardly surprising. From the point of view of combat

A Seafire wing in it's vertical frame showing the wing 'breaks' for carrier operation.

effectiveness no better choice could have been made than the two most outstanding and heavily-armed fighters of the day. Both of these aircraft were adapted for carrier-operation by the fitting of a deck-arrester hook and spools for catapult launching, and in this form they performed invaluable service against long-range enemy aircraft during the earlier, critical phases of the Battle of the Atlantic.

In the later war years the Spitfire, or the Seafire, to give it its Fleet Air Arm name, appeared as a complete naval conversion with folding wings - a surprising metamorphosis indeed for an aircraft originally designed as an out-and-out land-based fighter. Such a development was desirable in a carrier-based aircraft, and became a matter of urgency with the introduction of the small escort carriers which were brought into commission to supplement the large fleet carriers.

The introduction of a hinged joint into an established design of fighter wing was a modification which would hardly be viewed with great enthusiasm at any time. In most fighter wings it was necessary to accommodate so much equipment that the normal structure was very much broken up. The basic Spitfire wing was no exception to this rule, as it housed the outward-retracting undercarriage-leg as well as the machine-gun and cannon armament, with its associated ammunition-boxes and magazines. The Spitfire main spar was also regarded as something of an obstacle to the successful accomplishment of so drastic a surgical operation. Nevertheless, the decision was made to introduce the folding wing, and the necessary modifications in design were completed in a period of some three weeks.

Two hinged joints were introduced into the original fixed wing, with the result that the span of 36ft. 10 inch span was considerably reduced. The main joint was made near the edge of the wheel well, while the outboard joint corresponded to the attachment line of the wing-tip in the original wing.

As the tip was always built as a separate unit, there was a natural division in the structure and the introduction of a hinged joint at this point was not such a basic modification - principally a matter of substituting hinge fittings, with a suitable locking device, for the original attachment brackets. At the main joint, however, the hinge entailed the division of the forward main and rear subsidiary spars as well as the modification of the rib structure.

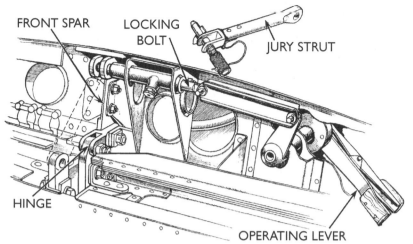

FRONT SPAR   LOCKING   JURY STRUT
              BOLT

HINGE

OPERATING LEVER

A detail sketch of the wingtip joint and locking mechanism on the front spar. The position of the jury strut for securing the wing in the folded position is shown by the dotted line.

Of these alterations the most fundamental was the division of the main spar, though the section of the rear spar between the fuselage attachment and the main hinge joint was considerably strengthened.

The Seafire mainplane structure was not notably adaptable to sub-assembly breakdown, though the introduction of the folding wing imposed a measure of compulsory division into components. In general, the basic structure was the same as the Spitfire. Smaller sub-assemblies included the cannon-bay structure, the top-surface structure over the wheel-well and what was known as No. 3 sub-assembly, which included interspar ribs 14 to 16 with the associated section of the rear spar.

The strengthened portion of the rear spar, inboard of the main joint, was of I-section built up from a web- plate and two pairs of L-section pressings riveted together, with local reinforcing plates at the root. This section and the outboard portions that remained, as in the Spitfire, a built-up channel, were assembled almost entirely by female workers.

The No.1 assembly, the portion of the Seafire wing inboard of the main joint in the assembly fixture.

The main assembly fixture for the Seafire wing was practically identical with that used for the Spitfire, with the addition of locations for the main hinge-joint fittings on front and rear spars. As a structure the fixture may be described as an enlarged version of that use for the No. 1 assembly. It was an open frame of structural-steel channels with the top member sloped to conform to the sweep forward of the rear spar. The end columns of the fixture carried locations for the fuselage joint pick-ups at one end and for the wing-tip fittings on the front and rear spars at the other.

Locations for the fittings of the main hinge joint were mounted on a pedestal set into the floor for the front spar, and for the rear spar on the post mounted between this pedestal and the top beam of the fixture. This beam also carried locations for the aileron hinge brackets on ribs 14 and 19 and a boundary location for the outboard flap rib.

A dummy flap, consisting of a steel tube (representing the flap spar) with a series of projecting steel bars which served as height locations for the recessed trailing-edge strip, was mounted between the outboard flap-rib location and the end column of the fixture, for the purpose of positioning the trailing edge structure aft of the rear spar.

Above: One of the wing main assembly fixtures showing the leading edge sections in position.

Left: the interspar and trailing edge structure ready for the application of skin plating.

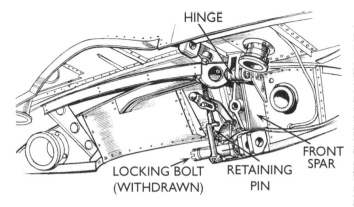

HINGE

FRONT SPAR

LOCKING BOLT (WITHDRAWN)   RETAINING PIN

The Seafire F Mk III was the first true carrier adaptation of the Spitfire design. It was developed from the Seafire Mk IIC, but incorporated manually folding wings, allowing more of these aircraft to be spotted on deck or in the hangars below. This version used the more powerful Merlin 55 (F Mk III and FR Mk III) or Merlin 55M (L Mk III), driving the same four-bladed propeller unit used by the IIC series; the Merlin 55M was another version of the Merlin modified to give maximum performance at low altitude. Other modifications that were made on the Spitfire made their way to the Seafire including a slim Aero-Vee air filter and six-stack ejector type exhausts. In addition the shorter barreled, lightweight Hispano Mk V cannon were introduced during production as were overload fuel tank fittings in the wings. This Mark was built in larger numbers than any other Seafire variant; of the 1,220 manufactured, Westland built 870 and Cunliffe Owen 350. In 1947 12 Mk IIIs were stripped of their naval equipment by Supermarine and delivered to the Irish Air Corps.

After the Mk III series the next Seafire variant to appear was the F Mk XV, which was powered by a Griffon VI driving a Rotol propeller. Designed in response to Specification N.4/43, this appeared to be a navalised Spitfire F Mk XII; in reality the Mk XV was an amalgamation of a strengthened Seafire III airframe and wings with the wing fuel tanks, retractable tailwheel, larger elevators and broad-chord 'pointed' rudder of the Spitfire VIII.

Left: drilling the flanges of ribs 8 and 10 for the Oddie fasteners which secured the Seafire's cannon-access door.

Right: removing the heads of the leading edge skin attachment rivets to give a flush surface.

Right: the main joint on the reat spar consisted of a simple hinge fitting. This drawing shows the strengthened construction of the inboard spar rear section.

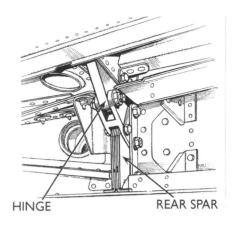

HINGE   REAR SPAR

Below: marking out the cut line on the leading edge skin panels. whilst on the assembly fixture. The leading edges were later removed, cut and trimmed down to size to these marked lines and finally de-burred.

Below right: the cut line for the skin panels on the upper surface of the wing was marked out from a large template mounted in the fixture. After the panels were marked out and cut, they were taken off for burr removal and dimpling.

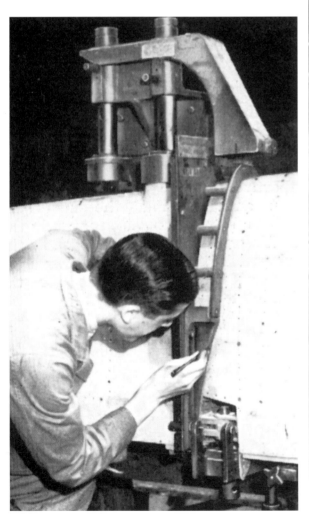

A complete starboard Seafire mainplane ready for removal from the main fixture.

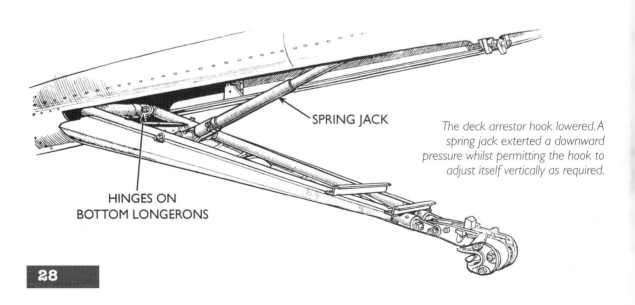

SPRING JACK

HINGES ON
BOTTOM LONGERONS

The deck arrestor hook lowered. A
spring jack exterted a downward
pressure whilst permitting the hook to
adjust itself vertically as required.

After all the fixture stages were completed the entire wing was placed on a wheeled stand for the final assembly operations.

Seafires were also made under sub-contract by Folland Aircraft Ltd of Southamption. This view below shows the Seafire mainplane assembly area with the fixture stages on the right and left, with a double line of final assembly trollies in between.

A view of one of the Folland shops showing leading-edge assembly in progress. In the immediate foreground nose ribs were being assembled to the spars. Farther back the fitting of leading edge skin plating is in progress. In the background were the fixtures for mainplane assembly.

Folland Aircraft, Ltd. had been engaged principally upon subcontract manufacture of aircraft components. As one of the Seafire group the firm was responsible for the production of stern portions (stern fuselage and empennage), mainplanes and the front-spar fuselage frame, known universally to those familiar with the Spitfire or Seafire structure as Frame 5. In the manufacture of all these components, a carefully organised system of balanced assembly stages had been worked out to make the most efficient use of fixtures and labour force available.

Seafire F XVII SX336 showing the wings fully folded and the arrestor hook.

POWERED BY ROLLS-ROYCE

Early Rolls-Royce Merlins under construction at Derby.

The British airframe industry would have been nothing without the magnificent Rolls-Royce Merlin aero-engine. The Merlin was a liquid-cooled, V-12, piston aero engine of 27-litre capacity. Rolls-Royce Limited initially designed and built the engine as the PV-12 - PV standing for 'Private Venture'.

The PV-12 first ran in 1933 and, after a number of modifications - and a name change to 'Merlin' following RR's convention of naming their engines after birds of prey - the first production variants were built in 1936. A series of rapidly applied developments brought about by wartime needs markedly improved the engine's performance and durability.

Considered a British icon, the Merlin was one of the most successful aircraft engines of the World War II era, and many variants were built by Rolls-Royce in Derby, Crewe and Glasgow, as well as by Ford of Britain at their Trafford Park factory, near Manchester. The Packard V-1650 was a version of the Merlin built in the United States. Production ceased in 1950 after a total of almost 150,000 engines had been delivered.

Merlins were built up on stands that could be rotated for ease of access. Some stands allowed for the engine to be completely inverted.

Literally thousands of components went to make up a single R-R Merlin, from the smallest of washers to the large castings. Here the crankcase is fettled - that is cleaned after removal from the casting molds. Pre- and post-war Merlins were finished to a different standard than wartime engines, many of which were not polished at all, just painted black.

The Merlin II and III were the first main production versions of the engine. The Merlin III was manufactured with a 'universal' propeller shaft, allowing either De Havilland or Rotol propellers to be used.

The next major version was the XX which ran on 100 octane fuel. This allowed higher manifold pressures, achieved by increasing the boost from the centrifugal type supercharger. The Merlin XX made use of two-speed superchargers resulting in increased power at higher altitudes than previous versions.

The process of improvement continued, with later versions running on further-increased octane ratings, delivering ever higher power. By the end of the war the 'little' engine was delivering over 1,600 horsepower in common versions, and as much as 2,060 horsepower in the Merlin 130/131 versions.

Many of the early Merlins were hand built by two-man teams - later they were built more more on production line principals.

From a contemporary report: 'After being reassembled the engine is fitted to the test bed, again primed with hot oil, and run light for half an hour. Three electric starts and one hand start are then made- to check magnetos and a half-hour incremental running carried out up to maximum continuous cruising conditions on the same lines as the previous incremental test. During this time power and consumption checks are made to prove satisfactory functioning of the engine.

The engine is then run for 25 minutes at maximum continuous cruising conditions, followed by 5 minutes at maximum climbing conditions, single ignition checks are then taken.

The same reading of revolutions per minute and brake horsepower are taken every 15 minutes as during the endurance tests, and the engine is then passed through the same six check tests that were made at the end of the endurance test, and in addition to checking the power curve at rated altitude (100 octane fuel). The exhaust manifolds removed, carburation and each magneto checked for slow running, maximum speed 480 r.p.m. with brake set for maximum continuous cruising condition, then three accelerations are carried out.

The engine is then passed off and finally inspected, filters examined and oil drained from the engine. One engine in every ten must complete a rated boost curve with points at 3,000, 2,850, 2,600 2,400 and 2,200 r.p.m.

On final assembly all external locking devices are brought into use, namely, split pins, wire and locking plates. In the first place only internal and a few important external nuts and unions need be locked. Lastly, all external pipes are enameled and main units and accessories are touched up if necessary. After final testing, exhaust ports, sparking plug holes, air intakes and pipe connections are each blanked off and fresh oil poured into each cylinder head for protection. The engine is then ready for despatch'.

Above: later in the war Merlins were later built on completely rotatable stands on production lines that ran around the building.

Below: 'Engines are delivered to the test-house by road, one vehicle transporting four engines, each mounted on a castor-wheeled cradle. In the receiving bay, they are unloaded by a hoist, controlled by push-buttons, on to an overhead runway, then wheeled to position for preliminary attention. Two operatives in about one hour remove all sealing blanks and fit sparking-plugs, exhaust stubs and gauge adaptors in readiness for testing.'

Merlins were tested in individual cells, each fitted out with an hoist and adjustable platform lift for erecting and dismounting the engine. The engine itself was mounted on a circular steel fixture some four feet in diameter restrained by steel cable looped around its periphery.

A number of Serck coolers - the three circular objects seen below the engine on test - provided temperature regulation for lubricating oil and engine coolant. Immediately to the rear of these coolers was a 'depression box' that was connected to the carburettor which through a shutter device, allowed the simulation of different altitudes to be made.

Staging was provided on both side of the engine so that adjustments could be made while the engine was being run - definately a draughty job for the technican!

35

HUNDREDS OF HURRICANES

Original caption: Benefiting from the comparative simplicity of the fabric-covered girder structure which permits rapid installation of equipment. Hawker Aircraft are fast delivering Hurricane eight-gun fighters from their Kingston works. The Hurricane demonstrates how a well-tried structural principle can be adapted to modern military aircraft, making a fine showing against machines of advanced stressed-skin construction.

The Hawker Hurricane was a single-seat fighter aircraft that was designed and predominantly built by Hawker Aircraft for the RAF. Although largely overshadowed by the Supermarine Spitfire, the Hurricane became renowned during the Battle of Britain, accounting for 60% of the RAF's air victories in the battle, and served in all the major theatres of the Second World War.

The 1930s design evolved through several versions and adaptations, resulting in a series of aircraft which acted as interceptor-fighters, fighter-bombers - also called 'Hurribombers'- and ground support aircraft. Further versions known as the Sea Hurricane had modifications which enabled operation from ships. Some were converted as catapult-launched convoy escorts, known as 'Hurricats'. More than 14,000 Hurricanes were built by the end of 1944, including about 1,200 converted to Sea Hurricanes and some 1,400 built in Canada by the Canada Car and Foundry.

Construction of the first prototype, K5083, began in August 1935 incorporating the PV-12 Merlin engine. Completed sections of the aircraft were taken to Brooklands, where Hawkers had an assembly shed, and re-assembled on 23 October 1935. Ground testing and taxi trials took place over the following two weeks, and on 6 November 1935, the prototype took to the air for the first time in the hands of Hawker's chief test pilot, Flight Lieutenant (later Group Captain) P. W. S. Bulman. Flight Lieutenant Bulman was assisted by two other pilots in subsequent flight testing; Philip Lucas flew some of the experimental test flights, while John Hindmarsh conducted the firm's production flight trials. Sammy Wroath, who was the founding Commandant of the Empire Test Pilot School, was the RAF test pilot for the Hurricane and his enthusiastic endorsement helped get it into production.

The maiden flight of the first production Hurricane, powered by a Merlin II engine, took place on 12 October 1937. The first four aircraft to enter service with the RAF joined 111 Sqn at RAF Northolt the following December. By the outbreak of the Second World War, nearly 500 Hurricanes had been produced, and had equipped eighteen squadrons.

Characteristic features of the Hurricane construction are well brought out in this view of the assembly. The centre-section is supported on adjustable trestles, the fuselage then being lowered into position; the alignment is checked by measuring the diagonals as seen here before the whole lot is bolted up.

Applying the fabric covering to the fuselage of a Hawker Hurricane. This extends forward from the sternpost to a point level with the pilot's seat.

The Hurricane was ordered into production in June 1936, mainly due to its relatively simple construction and ease of manufacture. As war was looking increasingly likely, and time was of the essence in providing the RAF with an effective fighter aircraft, it was unclear if the more advanced Spitfire would enter production smoothly, while the Hurricane used well-understood manufacturing techniques. This was true for service squadrons as well, who were experienced in working on and repairing aircraft whose construction employed the same principles as the Hurricane, and the simplicity of its design enabled the improvisation of some remarkable repairs in squadron workshops. The Hurricane was also significantly cheaper than the Spitfire, requiring 10,300 man hours to produce rather than 15,200 for the Spitfire.

Initially, the wing structure consisted of two steel spars, and was also fabric-covered. Several fabric-wing Hurricanes were still in service during the Battle of Britain, although a good number had had their wings replaced during servicing or after repair. Changing the wings only required three hours' work per aircraft. An all-metal, stressed-skin wing of duraluminium was introduced in April 1939 and was used for all of the later marks. Metal skinned wings allowed a diving speed that was 80 mph higher than the fabric-covered ones. The great advantage of the metal-covered wings over the fabric ones was that the metal ones could carry far greater stress loads without needing so much structure beneath.

The simplicity of its open-girder structure not only enables the Hawker Hurricane eight-gun single-seater fighter to be built rapidly in large numbers, but greatly facilitates the installation of its complex military equipment. In view of the speeds now being attained by fighters, and considering the limitations of fabric covering, it is to be doubted if any future single-seater fighter will be able to benefit likewise.

So said the original caption to this picture. One of Sydney Camm's priorities was to provide the pilot with good all round visibility. To this end, the cockpit was mounted reasonably high in the fuselage, creating a distinctive 'hump-backed' silhouette. Pilot access to the cockpit was aided by a retractable 'stirrup' mounted below the trailing edge of the port wing. This was linked to a spring-loaded hinged flap which covered a handhold on the fuselage, just behind the cockpit. When the flap was shut, the footstep retracted into the fuselage. In addition, both wingroots were coated with strips of non-slip material.

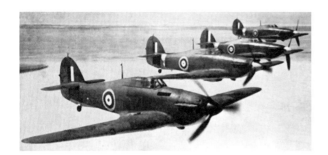

During 1940, Lord Beaverbrook, who was the Minister of Aircraft Production, established an organisation in which a number of manufacturers were seconded to repair and overhaul battle-damaged Hurricanes. The Civilian Repair Organisation also overhauled battle-weary aircraft, which were later sent to training units or to other air forces.

In all, some 14,000 Hurricanes and Sea Hurricanes were produced. The majority of Hurricanes were built by Hawker, with Hawker's sister company, the Gloster Aircraft Company, making 2,750. The Austin Aero Company built 300. Canada Car and Foundry in Fort William, Ontario, Canada, was responsible for production of 1,400 Hurricanes, known as the Mk X.

A general view of the Hurricane assembly shop. Machines are seen in the background coming up to the covering and doping shop, and, in the foreground, returning after these processes have been completed.

PZ865, the last Hurricane ever built during construction at Langley. The overhead banner proudly portrays the battle-honours won by the design.

The last Hurricane ever built, PZ865, rolled off the production line at Langley, Buckinghamshire, in the summer of 1944 with the inscription 'The Last of the Many' on her port and starboard sides. The aircraft was almost immediately purchased back from the Air Ministry by Hawkers and initially mothballed, before being employed as a company communications and test aircraft. In 1950, wearing the civilian registration G-AMAU, it was entered in the King's Cup Air Race by HRH Princess Margaret. Flown by Group Captain Peter Townsend, it achieved second place. During the 1960s, PZ865 was returned to its wartime camouflage scheme and was used as a company 'hack' and communications aircraft. It appeared in 'The Battle of Britain' film and also made numerous display appearances, often in the hands of the famous fighter pilot and test pilot Bill Bedford. After a complete overhaul, PZ865 was flown to Coltishall in March 1972 and given to the Memorial Flight by Hawker Siddeley. For many years the aircraft appeared as 'The Last of the Many' but eventually the inscription was removed and put on display in the BBMF headquarters.

TYPHOON TIME

The final stages of the Hawker Typhoon assembly line showing the engine feeder track on the left and in the foreground.

The Hawker Typhoon was a British single-seat fighter-bomber, produced by Hawker Aircraft. While the Typhoon was designed to be a medium-high altitude interceptor, and a direct replacement for the Hawker Hurricane, several design problems were encountered, and the Typhoon never completely satisfied this requirement. Other external events in 1940 prolonged the gestation of the Typhoon.

Nicknamed the Tiffy in RAF slang, the Typhoon's service introduction in mid-1941 was also plagued with problems, and for several months the aircraft faced a doubtful future. However, in 1941 the Luftwaffe brought the formidable Focke-Wulf Fw 190 into service: the Typhoon was the only fighter in the RAF inventory capable of catching the Fw 190 at low altitudes and, as a result, secured a new role as a low-altitude interceptor. Through the support of pilots such as Roland Beamont the Typhoon also established itself in roles such as night-time intruder and long-range fighter. From late 1942 the Typhoon was equipped with bombs; from late 1943 ground attack rockets were added to the Typhoon's armoury. Using these two weapons, the Typhoon became one of the Second World War's most successful ground-attack aircraft.

A line of Typhoon main plane assembly fixtures.

Even before the new Hurricane was rolling off the production lines in March 1937, Sydney Camm had moved on to designing its replacement. This was to be a big fighter designed around the large and more powerful 24-cylinder Napier Sabre engine. The work proved useful when Hawker received Specification F.18/37 from the Air Ministry in January 1938 which asked for a fighter based on either the Sabre or the Rolls-Royce Vulture engine. Both engines used 24 cylinders and were designed to be able to deliver over 2,000 hp; the difference between the two was primarily in the arrangement of the cylinders – an H-block in the Sabre and an X-block in the Vulture.

The two designs became known as the 'R' and 'N'- from the initial of the engine manufacturer - and were very similar; the Vulture-powered R type, which became known as the Tornado, had a rounder nose profile and a ventral radiator, whereas the Sabre-powered N - the Typhoon - had a flatter deck and a chin-mounted radiator. The basic design of both was a combination of traditional Hawker and more modern construction techniques; the front fuselage structure, from the engine mountings to the rear of the cockpit, was made up of bolted and welded duralumin or steel tubes, while the rear fuselage was a flush-riveted, semi-monocoque structure. The forward fuselage and cockpit skinning was made up of large, removable duralumin panels, allowing easy external access to the engine and engine accessories and most of the important hydraulic and electrical equipment.

Right: a Hawker Typhoon in flight.

The first flight of the first Typhoon prototype, P5212, made by Hawker's Chief test Pilot Philip Lucas from Langley, was delayed until 24 February 1940 because of problems with the development of the Sabre engine. Although unarmed for its first flights, P5212 later carried an armament of 12 .303 in Browning machine guns, set in groups of six in each outer wing panel; this was the armament fitted to the first 110 Typhoons, known as the Typhoon IA. P5212 also had a small tail-fin, triple exhaust stubs and no wheel doors fitted to the centre-section. On 9 May 1940 the prototype suffered from a mid-air structural failure, at the joint between the forward fuselage and rear fuselage, just behind the pilot's seat. Philip Lucas could see daylight through the split but, instead of baling out, he was able to land the stricken Typhoon and was later awarded the George Medal.

Drilling jigs made of steel strips and in three sections are located over the interspar structure to drill the rib flanges for the attachment of the skin plating.

As a result of the delays the second prototype, P5216, first flew on 3 May 1941: P5216 carried an armament of four 20 mm Hispano Mk II cannon, each with 140 rounds per gun and was the first prototype of the Typhoon IB series. In the interim between construction of the first and second prototypes the Air Ministry had given Hawker orders to proceed with the construction of 1,000 of the new fighters. It was felt that the Vulture engine was more promising, so the order covered 500 Tornadoes and 250 Typhoons, with the balance to be decided once the two had been compared. As a result of good progress by Gloster the first production Typhoon, R7576, was first flown on 27 May 1941 by Michael Daunt, just three weeks after the second prototype.

An undercarriage actuation test in progress on a set of port and starboard Typhoon wings.

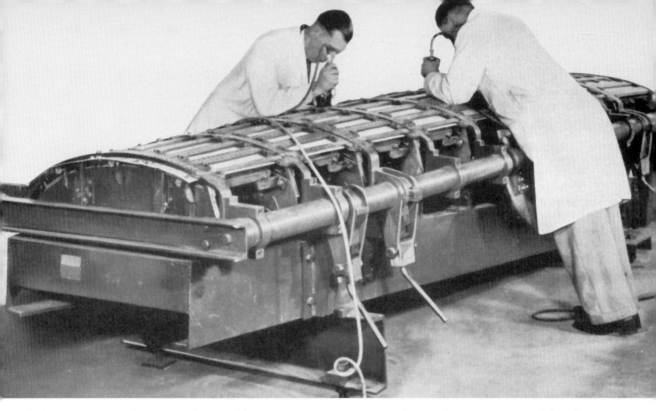

Drilling in progress in the main jig for one of the quarter monocoque sections. Quarter frames, stringers and skin plating are all located in the jig and and drilled through the gate.

The assembly fixture in which the Typhoon rear fuselage quarter sections are aligned and prepared for rivetting.

Typhoon Production: the fuselage assembly track from the finishing end.

In 1941 the Spitfire Vs which equipped the bulk of Fighter Command squadrons were outclassed in combat with the Focke-Wulf Fw.190 and were suffering heavy losses. The Typhoon was rushed into service with 56 and 609 Sqns in the summer of 1941 in an attempt to counter the Fw.190. This decision proved to be a disaster, and several Typhoons were lost to unknown causes.

The Air Ministry began to consider halting production of the Typhoon. The in-flight tail failure was eventually identified, albeit only because one pilot survived and was able to explain what had happened; Mod 286 was a partial remedy, although there were still failures right up to the end of the Typhoon's service life. The Sabre engine was also a constant source of problems, notably in colder weather, when it was very difficult to start.

The Typhoon did not begin to mature as a reliable aircraft until the end of 1942, when its good qualities became apparent. It was extremely fast, tough and capable. During late 1942 and early 1943, the Typhoon squadrons on the South Coast were finally effective in countering the Luftwaffe's 'tip and run' low-level nuisance raids, shooting down a score or more fighter-bomber Fw.190s.

To counter such attacks Typhoon squadrons kept at least one pair of aircraft flying continuously on standing patrols over the South coast, with another pair kept at 'readiness'; ready to take off within two minutes, throughout daylight hours. These sections of Typhoons flew at 500 feet or lower, with enough height to spot and then intercept the incoming enemy fighter-bombers. These tactics were successful during early 1943.

A distinctive feature of the Typhoon was the underslung radiator.

The drill jig for the bottom, port and starboard sides of the radiator fairing.

The fixture in which the side and bottom unit of the fairing is drilled for assembly with the front section

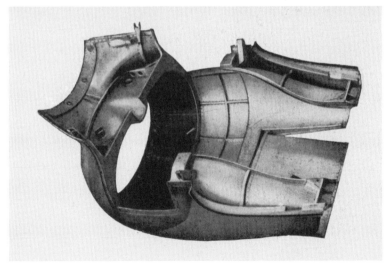

The completed fairing for the Typhoon showing the internal structure for oil and engine coolant radiators.

Initial jig assembly of the Instrument Panel in the fuselage decking.

Workers installing the electrical wiring in the decking unit of the Typhoon. This work is broken down into sucessive stanges.

The rear monococque portion of the fuselage with the pilot's rear armour plate already installed.

As with all front line RAF aircraft, the Typhoon was modified and updated regularly, so that a 1945 production example looked quite different from one built in 1941. In the last months of the war a number of older aircraft were taken out of storage and overhauled, sometimes seeing active service for the first time.

The first problem encountered with the Typhoon after its entry into service was the seepage of carbon monoxide fumes into the cockpit. In an attempt to alleviate this, longer exhaust stubs were fitted in November 1941 ('Mod 239'), and at about the same time the port cockpit doors were sealed. The Pilot's Notes for the Typhoon recommended that 'Unless Mod. No. 239 has been embodied it is most important that oxygen be used at all times as a precaution against carbon monoxide poisoning'.

The forward girder fuselage was fitted out with all required equipment before installing to the rest of the aircraft on the assembly track.

Original caption: The main planes were brought up to the fuselage on trolleys which support them in the assembly position at the correct height for bolting on to the spar fittings of the forward girder fuselage.

The Typhoon was first produced with forward-opening side doors (complete with wind-down windows), with a transparent 'roof' hinged to open to the left. The first 162 Typhoons featured a built-up metal-skinned fairing behind the pilot's armoured headrest; the mast for the radio aerial protruded through the fairing. From mid- to late 1941 the solid metal aft canopy fairing was replaced with a transparent structure - later nicknamed 'The Coffin Hood' - the pilot's head armour plate was modified to a triangular shape and the side cut-outs were fitted with armoured glass; the first production Typhoon to be fitted with this new structure was R7803. All earlier aircraft were quickly withdrawn and modified.

From early 1942 a rear-view mirror was mounted in perspex blisters moulded into the later 'car-door' canopy roofs. This modification was not very successful, because the mirror was subject to vibration. Despite the new canopy structure the pilot's visibility was still restricted by the heavy frames and the clutter of equipment under the rear canopy; from August 1943, as an interim measure, pending the introduction of the new 'bubble' canopy, the aerial mast and its associated bracing was removed and replaced with a whip aerial further back on the rear fuselage.

Starting in January 1943 R8809 was used to test a new, clear, one piece sliding 'bubble' canopy and its associated new windscreen structure which had slimmer frames which provided a far superior field of view to the car-door type. From November 1943 all production aircraft, starting with JR333, were to be so fitted. However, the complex modifications required to the fuselage and a long lead time for new components to reach the production line meant that it took some time before the new canopy became standard. In order to have as many Typhoons of 2nd TAF as possible fitted before 'Operation Overlord' conversion kits were produced and Gloster, Hawker and Cunliffe-Owen modified older Typhoons still fitted with the car-door canopy.

NAPIER SABRE POWER

The Napier Sabre was a H format-24-cylinder, liquid cooled, sleeve valve, piston aero engine, designed by Major Frank Halford and built by Napier & Son. The engine evolved to become one of the most powerful inline piston aircraft engines in the world, developing from 2,200 horsepower in its earlier versions to 5,500 hp in late-model prototypes

The first operational aircraft to use the Sabre were the Hawker Typhoon and Hawker Tempest; however, the first actual aircraft powered by the Sabre was the Napier-Heston Racer, which was designed to capture the world speed record. Other aircraft using the Sabre were the Martin-Baker MB 3 prototype and one of the Hawker Fury prototypes. Later it became used in the early production of the Blackburn Firebrand.

Left: the front end of a Sabre showing the four compound reduction gears through which the two crankshaft pinions drove the airscrew shaft.

Napier first decided to develop a 24 cylinder, liquid cooled engine capable of producing at least 2,000 hp in late 1935. Although the company continued with the opposed 'H' layout of their earlier Dagger, the new design positioned the cylinder blocks horizontally and was to use sleeve valves. All the accessories were grouped accessibly above and below the cylinder blocks, rather than being at the front and rear of the engine as in most contemporary designs.

The first Sabre engines were ready for testing in January 1938, although they were limited to 1,350 hp. By March they were already passing tests at 2,050 hp and by June 1940 when the Sabre passed the Air Ministry 100-hour type-test, the first production-ready versions were delivering 2,200 hp from their 37 litres. By the end of the year, they were producing 2,400 hp. To put this in perspective, the contemporary 1940 Rolls-Royce Merlin II was generating just over 1,000 hp

Problems started to arise as soon as production started in volume. Until then the prototype engines had been hand-assembled by Napier craftsmen and it proved to be difficult to adapt it to assembly line production techniques. In particular, the sleeves often failed, leading to seized cylinders. After testing a whole range of materials and manufacturing methods techniques a process of nitriding and lapping the sleeves helped resolve the problem.

By 1944, the Sabre V was delivering 2,400 hp consistently, and the reputation of the engine started to improve. This was the last version to see service, powering the Hawker Typhoon and its derivative, the Tempest.

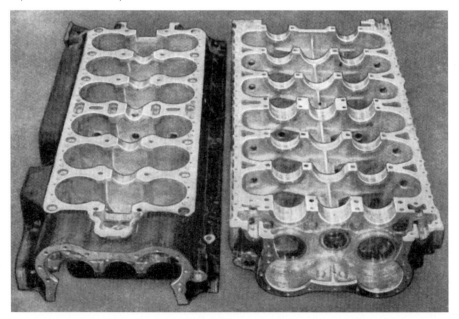

An overall view of Napier's crankcase machining department. Each line of machines is flanked by a roller conveyor.

The assembly shop at Napiers was divided into six main departments comprising sub-assembly first-build, engine first-build, engine strip and sub-assembly rebuild after test, engine rebuild for final test, and packing and despatch: the sixth department was reserved for special work and building for retests.

The sub-assembly first-build department was sub-divided into a number of self-contained sections for building and rig testing the various units. In all, there were seven main units comprising the crankcase complete with crankshafts and con-rods; cylinder blocks complete with worm shafts, sleeves, worm wheel cranks, supercharger drive and gear shafts; nosepiece assembly comprising the airscrew shaft, layshafts and carrier plate; auxiliary drive case; bottom cover and sump, including coolant pumps and petrol pump drive; supercharger; various small components such as pistons, junk heads, oil filter, and hand turning gear.

Left: balancing the sleeves and timing the port opening.

Part of the cylinder block assembly line, with each block mounted on rotatable fixtures.

Once the engine had been on static test it was returned to the assembly shop for complete strip and examination, during which each component was checked and its history details logged. Rebuilding took place in the same sequence as that followed on the first-build line, and the re-assembled engine returned to the test house for final test. A short motoring period was carried out to satisfy certain assembly standards, ignition-plugs were fitted and 'running in' again commenced. During the final test-running period was reduced to one hour, at the completion of which tuning, auxiliary pressures and temperatures were again carefully checked. When all adjustments were satisfactorily completed the previous test conditions were again carried out, finishing with the acceleration test. The engine was then removed and the sump filters re-checked prior to removal for packing and despatch.

The last stage of assembly when all pipes and ignition control harnesses were fitted. This was followed by air, water and oil tests of the various engine passages.

THE TEMPEST

A family likeness may be expected to appear in successive designs of the same company, but a more than usual close resemblance existed between the Hawker Tempest V and the Typhoon. Indeed, almost the only difference from a casual inspection was in the mainplane, straight-tapered and of rather deep section in the Typhoon, much thinner and of semi-elliptical planform in the Tempest. This difference accounted for, without justifying, the description of the Tempest as '...the Typhoon with a new wing,' but was by no means the only difference between the two aircraft.

As its appearance suggested, the Tempest originated in a decision to improve the aerodynamic qualities of the Typhoon with particular reference to the wing. Design work on the Typhoon began in 1937 when little was known about the phenomena and effects of compressibility which later assumed such importance with the great advance in speeds. A high-lift aerofoil with the natural accompaniment of a fairly thick section was selected for the Typhoon, partly because of the increased wing-loading - 40 lb./sq. ft. for the Typhoon as against 25 lb./sq. ft. for the Hurricane - and partly from structural and space considerations.

The wings of a fighter must necessarily be used to accommodate a large amount of equipment, and at the time it was necessary to meet a specific requirement that all fuel should be carried in the wings. As the Napier Sabre engine would develop a large increase in power over that of any existing unit, it was necessary, in order to give the Typhoon adequate range, to find space for a much larger fuel supply than had hitherto been necessary on a single-engined fighter. Provision had also to be made for mounting the armament and accommodating the undercarriage legs. In connection with the undercarriage, a minor contributory factor was the limit on tyre pressures which existed at that time. This factor in itself imposed certain minimum limits on the size of the tyre and had an influence in determining the amount of space required to accommodate the retracted wheel.

With increasing knowledge of compressibility, the need became evident for a modified wing section to improve the performance of the Typhoon in the higher speed range and take the utmost advantage of the higher power of the engine. An intensive examination of the problem began in 1940 and a special Hawker aerofoil section was evolved, much thinner than the original Typhoon wing.

Tempest port and starboard trailing sections of the wing - aft of the rear spar - were assembled in large, paired up vertical fixtures.

In order to compensate for the smaller space available for fuel in the new wing and to extend the range of the aircraft it was decided to fit a large tank in the fuselage forward of the cockpit. An extra bay to accommodate the tank became necessary in the girder portion of the fuselage with the natural result that the engine and the centre of gravity were moved forward and extra stabilising area was required in the form of a larger fin and tailplane. The sum of these modifications was, in effect, a new type of aircraft and in 1942, it was decided to give the name Tempest to what had until then been known as Typhoon II. The prototype Tempest was flown in September, 1942, and the first production aircraft in June 1943.

The Tempest II, the radial-engined version of the aircraft, derived from a prototype Tornado, the corresponding design to the Typhoon originally fitted with a Rolls-Royce 24-cylinder Vulture engine. In 1941, an experimental conversion of the Tornado prototype was made and a Bristol Centaurus radial engine was installed in place of the Rolls-Royce engine.

Right: inboard portions of the trailing edge assembly, showing the fixtures in position for locating the apertures of the cannon magazine and gun-bay access doors.

The Tempest II fitted with the Centaurus V radial engine.

The Tempest II was remarkable for the manner in which the very compact, but still massive, 18 cylinder 2,500 h.p.-plus Centaurus V engine had been embodied in the nose of an aircraft of truly superlative aerodynamic cleanness. A special exhaust and cooling system were designed by Hawker Aircraft, Ltd. for the installation and the engine, as might be expected, was very tightly cowled. Separate pipes from each cylinder led the exhaust back to a point behind the engine where they ejected through the sides of the cowling. Control of the cooling air past the engine was effected by sliding gills just aft of the exhaust.

The oil-cooler and carburettor air intakes were very neatly arranged in the leading edge of the wing close to the fuselage and, with the large spinner, completd a most attractive power-unit installation. The prototype Tempest II was flown in June 1943 and the first production aircraft in September 1944.

Apart from the engine mountings, the forward fuselage is exacly the same as the Sabre engined machine.

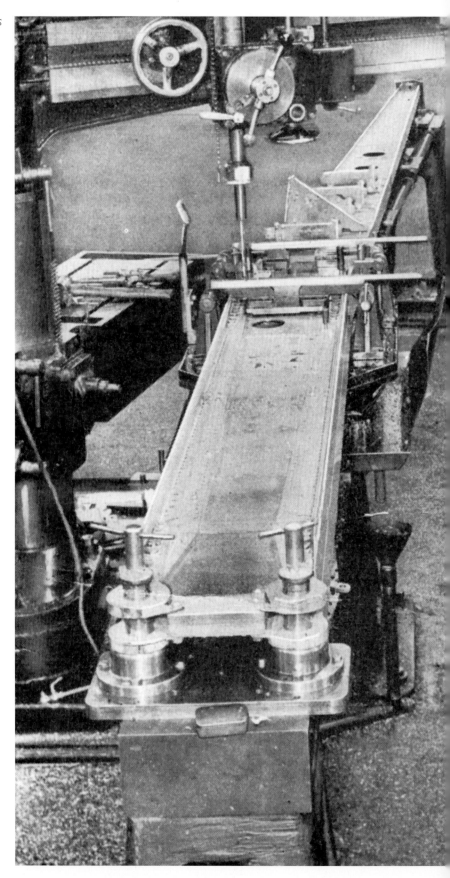

The final drill-jig in which the holes were reamed in the intermediate section of the Tempest spar for the butt-strap joint with the root section.

Production of the Tempest's leading-edge assembly fell into two main parts, the first - the assembly of the nosing outboard of the dihedral joint - was done in large trunnion-mounted fixtures. In this section of the leading edge, the nose ribs were designated by letters from A to O. The three at the inboard end, A, B and C, were assembled as a small unit in a separate fixture.

The main fixture consisted of two cast-iron columns with trunnion-bearings for the main assembly platform, which, in its turn, was a massive cast-iron member ribbed longitudinally to counteract bending and bolted at the ends to the trunnion brackets. These brackets carried adjustable balance-weights to reduce effort needed in handling the platform. It was possible to locate the platform in three different positions by indexing pins inserted through bushings in the end columns into bushed holes in each of the trunnion brackets.

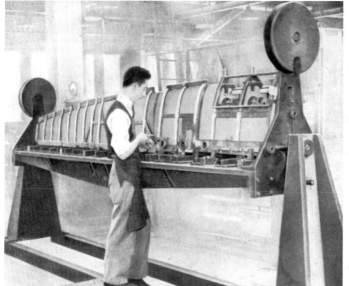

At intervals along the platform representing the rib stations were set up a series of vertical templates which serve as locations for tlie nose ribs. Longitudinal strips along the bases of the template located the edges of the skin-plating. Each rib was located on a tooling-hole near the tip and by the spar-attachment angles at the root.

Top: The first stage of leading edge assembly - The nose ribs have been located and clamped at their respective positions.

Middle: drilling the skin panels and nose-rib flanges from cage-type jigs located over the skin.

Bottom: Rivetting the skin to the ribs in the third stage of Tempest leading edge assembly. The fixture has been swung round to bring the assembly into the horizontal positition for ease of working.

Large paired-up fixtures accommodating both port and starboard wings were used for ther assembly of the Tempest wing as a complete unit.

In the main assembly fixture the basic structure of the wing was completed. This fixture resembled that for the trailing-edge structure and accommodated both port and starboard units. It was similar to the earlier assembly fixtures used for Hurricane and Typhoon wing assembly. Three large cast-iron columns carried the main pick-ups and were bridged by a large-diameter tubular top-beam. These tubular members in the wing assembly fixtures were found to be essential in order to maintain rigidity as the wing structure was sufficiently strong to distort the fixture if ordinary structural-steel sections were used.

Location for port and starboard front and rear-spar root-fittings were mounted on the centre column. The two outer columns, on which the wing-tip locations were mounted, were in line with each other but offset in relation to the centre column. This arrangement was adopted to simplify the build and could be dropped clear of the end of the wing and permit it to be withdrawn almost longitudinally immediately the root locations had been freed.

Leading edge and trailing sections in the main assembly fixture with the interspar ribs in position.

The building of the aileron commenced with the riveting of the bottom surface stringers to the underside skin, and the ribs and top-surface stringers to the top-surface skin. For each surface the work is divided into two stages, the first of which was the drilling of the skin and structural members together in a single jig. Each rib was located by tooling holes, one in the web near the trailing end and one in the forward spar attachment flange, and held by quick-action toggle-clamps against location blocks at the proper stations.

Owing to the thinness of the skin plating and the consequent difficulties of obtaining a surface free from panting and buckling if the normal methods of handling were adopted, panels were pre-stretched on a tubular frame before being located on the jig. Both ends of the panel were turned over to form a right angled flange. Holes were pierced in each end, and the skin was clamped by pins inserted through these holes. At the tip end of the skin the pins were inserted directly into the tubular frame, and at the root end the skin was clamped between strips in a frame carried on adjusting screws. By turning the screws the skin can be stretched to remove any waves or any tendency to buckle.

The same drill jig with a skin panel tacked to the rib structure and ready for removal to the riveting stage.

A Tempest port wing on one of the mobile final assembly stands showing the undercarriage-leg wheel bay and the tank bay templates in position ready for the fitting of the underside skin.

Before assembly to the fuselage a pair of wings- complete by now with an undercarriage leg on each side - was mounted on a test stand for actuation tests on a rig that mimicked the cockpit controls and indicators.

WOOD OR METAL BLADES?

Fighters could not fight if they had no propellers - or 'aircrews' as they known.

Wartime shortages of light alloys has greatly accelerated the development of wood blades, but apart from the conservation of material, this type possess various other advantages by comparison with metal. Reduced weight, the ease and wide scope of carrying out repairs, a most important asset in wartime, and the possibility of producing special types rapidly without the need for expensive forming dies.

Rotol Airscrews Ltd., amongst others adopted the wood blade, and with airscrew hubs produced by this Company the adoption was made possible by the fundamental design. It embodied a hollow, steel root adaptor capable of holding the base of the blade in a compressed condition and so providing the degree of support necessary to meet stresses imposed in flight. Considerable numbers of Rotol airscrews with wood blades were in service on fighter, bomber and trainer types of aircraft. The standard of performance and reliability had been proved to be most satisfactory.'

The picture above shows the wooden planks being laid out prior to gluing and compressing. The area of the blade where the hub was to be formed remained under compression until the remainder of the glue dried as shown on the left.

All wood blades fitted to Rotol airscrews had to be covered : *Rotoloid* or *Rayloid* covering consisted of a nitro-cellulose sheet approximately 0.04 inches thick. *Schwarz* covering comprised cellulose acetate sheet of approximately 0.04in. thickness, reinforced with fabric. In this covering the leading edge was protected by a continuous brass sheath. Beneath this sheath and extending a little way behind it, was a reinforcing sheet of phosphor-bronze. *Jablo* covering consisted of a bronze gauze wrapped round the blade, on to which successive coats of *Jablo* synthetic resin enamel was sprayed.

Once the blades were carved to shape, each was held in an adjustable counter-balanced fixture for finishing and balancing. The delicate patterns created by the different timbers used for the laminations and carvings, so beautiful to see when exposed, were later hidden by the coverings.

Metal blades were manufactured broadly in the same way, starting with a blade blank.

Each blade root had to be turned, bored and screw-cut to fit into the hub. This was done on a conventional metal-turning lathe, but with a special support fixture that held the blade blank in the correct position for machining.

Once the hub end was completed, the two edges of the blade could be simultaneously milled by this Sundestrand profiler followng a master template held behind the blade being machined. The suspended weight visible to the right ensured that a constant pressure was applied to both the follower and milling cutters.

A small amount of metal was left on each edge for final machining when the blade profile was created.

Machining operations on the faces and edges of root sections of a blade, using a finished item as master. The circular follower running around the top blade was exactly the same diameter as the cutter machining the lower one to ensure the correct one-to-one relationship. Each blade was locked into the device holding both blades which is rotationally electrically driven while the machine table moves the entire complex from left to right.

After machining, a special bench holding a, clamping fixture and gauge holder was used for checking the blade profile at various positions.

The blade holder could be indexed around to specific positions so that the inspector could use the different templates - some of which can be seen lying on the right hand side of the bench - to check that the shape was correct.

Once each blade was machined, all marks left by the machine tools had to be polished away and the blade then balanced.

Here the preliminary polishing and balancing operations is being done by a skilled operator using a powered rotary mop. The blade is held in an adjustable counterbalanced fixture.

AIRACOBRA FOR THE RAF!

RAF Bell P-39 Caribou fighters on the two main assembly lines at the Buffalo works. At each station is a stack of shelves carrying all materials needed at that point.

The Bell P-39 Airacobra was one of the principal American fighter aircraft in service when the United States entered World War Two. It was the first fighter in history with a tricycle undercarriage and the first to have the engine installed in the centre fuselage, behind the pilot. Although its mid-engine placement was innovative, the P-39 design was handicapped by the absence of an efficient turbo-supercharger, limiting it to low-altitude work. The P-39 was used with great success by the Soviet Air Force, who scored the highest number of individual kills attributed to any U.S. fighter type. Together with the derivative P-63 Kingcobra, these aircraft became the most successful mass-produced fixed-wing aircraft manufactured by Bell.

In 1940, the British Direct Purchase Commission in the US was looking for combat aircraft; they ordered 675 of the export version Bell Model 14 as the 'Caribou' on the strength of the company's representations on 13 April 1940. The British armament was two nose mounted 0.50 in machine guns, and four 0.303 inch Browning machine guns in the wings; the 37 mm gun was replaced by a 20 mm Hispano-Suiza.

British expectations had been set by performance figures established by the unarmed and unarmoured XP-39 prototype. The British production contract stated that a maximum speed of 394 mph (+/- 4%) was required at rated altitude. In acceptance testing, actual production aircraft were found to be capable of only 371 mph at 14,090 ft. To enable the aircraft to make the guarantee speed, a variety of drag reduction modifications were developed by Bell, after which the aircraft was about 200 pounds lighter. The second production aircraft (AH 571) reached 391 mph at 14,400 ft, in flight test. As this speed was within 1% of the guarantee, the aircraft was declared to have satisfied the contractual obligations, but none of the modifcations were applied to other production P-39s. Later testing of a standard production aircraft at the Aeroplane and Armament Experimental Establishment in Great Britain revealed a top speed of only 359 mph.

The British export models were renamed 'Airacobra' in 1941. A further 150 were specified for delivery under Lend-lease in 1941 but these were not supplied. The RAF took delivery in mid 1941 and found that performance of the non-turbo-supercharged production aircraft differed markedly from what they were expecting. Tests by the RAE at Boscombe Down showed the Airacobra reached 355 mph at 13,000 ft. The cockpit layout was criticised, and it was noted that the pilot would have difficulty in baling out in an emergency because the cockpit roof could not be jettisoned. The lack of a clear vision panel on the windscreen assembly meant that in the event of heavy rain the pilot's forward view would be completely obliterated; the pilot's notes advised that in this case the door windows would have to be lowered and the speed reduced to 150 mph.

A RAF P-39 fuselage with cabin attached nearing completion on the assembly line.

The fuselage 'chassis' for the P-39 was built in a different manner to all other aircraft of the day, with a strong lower half that carried all the main components.

Despite the obvious problems, the Airacobra was considered effective for low level fighter and ground attack work. The problems with gun and exhaust flash suppression and the compass could be fixed.

601 Squadron RAF was the only British unit to use the Airacobra operationally, receiving their first two examples on 6 August 1941. On 9 October, four Airacobras attacked enemy barges near Dunkirk, in the type's only operational action with the RAF. The squadron continued to train with the Airacobra during the winter, but a combination of poor serviceability and deep distrust of this unfamiliar fighter resulted in the RAF rejecting the type after just one combat mission. In March 1942, the unit re-equipped with Spitfires.

The Airacobras already in the UK, along with the remainder of the first batch being built in the US, were sent to the Soviet Air Force, the sole exception being AH574, which was passed to the Royal Navy and used for experimental work, including the first carrier landing by a tricycle undercarriage aircraft on 4 April 1945 on HMS *Pretoria Castle*, until it was scrapped on the recommendation of a visiting Bell test pilot in March 1946.

A Bell Airacobra in RAF markings.

Lines of cabin units on wheeled trolleys in the sub-assembly shop.

The Airacobra was one of the first production fighters to be conceived as a 'weapons system'; in this case the aircraft was designed around the 37mm T9 cannon. The 200 lb, 90 inch long weapon had to be rigidly mounted and fire parallel to and close to the centreline of the new fighter. It would be impossible to mount the weapon in the fuselage, firing through the propeller shaft as could be done with smaller 20mm cannon. Weight, balance and visibility problems meant that the cockpit could not be placed farther back in the fuselage, behind the engine and cannon. The solution adopted was to mount the cannon in the forward fuselage and the engine in the centre fuselage, directly behind the pilot's seat. The tractor propeller was driven via a 10-foot-long drive shaft which was made in two sections, incorporating a self-aligning bearing to accommodate fuselage deflection during violent manoeuvres. This shaft ran through a tunnel in the cockpit floor and was connected to a gearbox in the nose of the fuselage which, in turn, drove the three- or (later) four-bladed propeller via a short central shaft. The gearbox was provided with its own lubrication system, separate from the engine; in later versions of the Airacobra the gearbox was provided with some armour protection. The glycol-cooled radiator was fitted in the wing centre section, immediately beneath the engine; this was flanked on either side by a single drum shaped oil cooler. Air for the radiator and oil coolers was drawn in through intakes in both wing-root leading edges and was directed via four ducts to the radiator faces. The air was then exhausted through three controllable hinged flaps near the trailing edge of the centre section. Air for the carburettor was drawn in via a raised oval intake immediately aft of the rear canopy.

SMALL SCALE TRACK BUILDS

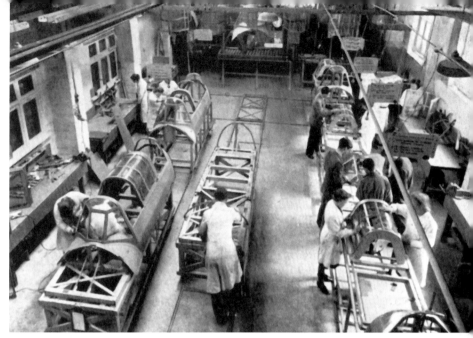

Just as British aircraft production was not just about huge production lines, British fighters could not operate without other aircraft operating in more lowly roles such as target tugs for gunnery practice.

The opinion of many production engineers that line- and track-assembly methods were only economical for large-scale production and could only be applied in workshops of considerable area was shown to be incorrect by the ingenious, but simple, track system installed by Metalair Ltd., for the assembly of Martinet cabin tops. The track installed fitted an area that measured only 68ft. by 26ft., the track equipment being of the most simple and practical nature, and the operations had been carefully planned and timed to ensure balanced production. To overcome lack of floorspace use was made of light overhead racks for storage and drying purposes.

There were two short tracks, each carrying three trucks: on one line were assembled the main details and the other was for final assembly and inspection. Joining the ends of the tracks were cross rails which, by means of a movable switch, allowed the trucks to be transferred to a central rail for return to the other end of their respective lines. By this simple method the trucks progressed with a circular movement, returning to the beginning of their track for loading.

Below left: one of the detail assembly trucks. It can be seen that the sliding hood fixture on the right is arranged to tilt to enable the drilling from the underside.

Below right: A final assembly truck. Part of the rear windscreen is on the right and the crash pylon in the centre were already in position. Note the truck is running in simple angle-iron rails.

Overhead racks, operated by light winches on which the detail components were suspended for drying after spraying and for short-term storage.

For ease of assembly the cabin top was divided into five main components, i.e., front windscreen, front sliding hood, centre fixed hood, rear sliding hood, and rear windscreen.   Each truck on the detail assembly line was arranged to accommodate two different components, one windscreen and a hood : in the case of the front windscreen, which required twice the assembly time of any of the other four items, the fixture was duplicated and the windscreen passed twice around the track before completion. By this means one front windscreen was completed in the same period as the other four components, thus maintaining balanced production.

Each truck was simply designed from light steel angles and strip, and incorporated the fixtures required for the particular component. Where necessary, the fixtures were arranged to swivel or turn over to provide access to the rear or underneath, and each incorporated its own drilling jig and locations. All screws and nuts were run up to a predetermined tension with portable electric equipment carried on each truck. There were three stations on each line, where three sets of operations were performed at each by four workers.

To maintain the workers' interest in the programme, special indicators and stage clocks were erected at the end of each line. From these the starting (left) and finishing (right) times of the current stage were shown, and every operator was able to see at a glance if the work was progressing according to schedule. As the trucks moved to new stages the clocks were reset by the foreman. On the same boards was given also the following information : (i) number of complete stages finished during the day and during the week up to date, and, below these, the total completed on the contract up to date. From this data the operators were always able to compute their piecework earnings, and were instantly aware if they were behind on their programme. Between the two pairs of indicating clocks was a board showing (top) the total number of stages which should be completed up to the end of the day to maintain the weekly target and the number actually completed up to date, during the current working week. This provided a quick comparison of target figures and actual output.

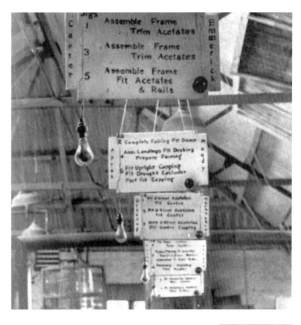

Instruction boards installed above each work station They carried the operators' names, jig or station number, and a red light came on to call the attention of the inspector when the work was completed.

A finished Miles Martinet cabin top, ready for removal from this sub-assembly line.

Over each workstation was a board bearing the workers' name, the stage number and the operations to be performed at that station. This provided a ready guide for any new personnel. The portion bearing the name was easily detachable should the operator leave or move to another station. Many of the staff had not undergone anything like a full apprenticeship and therefore trained to be capable of working in any department. Instead, given the pressure of war, many workers had been taken on and trained for one specific task.

Adjacent to each board was a red lamp which was switched on when the operations on the component were completed, this attracting the attention of the floor inspector who then examined the work. When all lights were illuminated the trucks moved on to the next station, the lights were switched off, and the end truck unloaded and returned, via the central rails, to the commencement of the track. At the side of the tracks were benches to which the parts were transferred from the trucks for certain operations, such as trimming, glazing, etc. The benches were fitted with racks for tools, details, and jigs for small sub-assemblies.

As the finished parts were removed at the end of the detail line they passed on to a spray booth for masking and painting, and were then dried and stored on overhead racks until required for final assembly. There were five of these racks made from light angle iron, each raised and lowered separately on steel cables by light winches. Drying was facilitated by warm air at rack level, which was fed through a duct from a furnace outside the building.

Right: Miles Martinet target tug HN861 in flight.

WHISPERING DEATH

A line of Beaufighters approaching completion. The ducts above each machine were part of the air-conditioning equipment.

The Bristol Type 156 Beaufighter, often referred to as simply the Beau, was a British long-range heavy fighter modification of the Bristol Aeroplane Company's earlier Beaufort torpedo bomber design. The name Beaufighter is a portmanteau of 'Beaufort' and 'fighter'.

Unlike the Beaufort, the Beaufighter had a long career and served in almost all theatres of war, first as a night fighter, then as a fighter bomber and eventually replacing the Beaufort as a torpedo bomber. A variant was built in Australia by the Department of Aircraft Production (DAP) and was known in Australia as the DAP Beaufighter.

The idea of a fighter development of the Beaufort was suggested to the Air Ministry by Bristol. The suggestion coincided with the delays in the development and production of the Westland Whirlwind cannon-armed twin-engine fighter. Bristol proopsed a fixed four cannon version and a turret fighter with twin cannons; the former was preferred by the Assistant Chief of the Air Staff. For fighter-like performance Bristol suggested their new Hercules engines in place of the Beaufort's Taurus.

Since the 'Beaufort Cannon Fighter' was a conversion of an existing design, development and production could be expected far more quickly than with a completely fresh design. Accordingly, the Air Ministry produced draft Specification F.11/37 written around Bristol's suggestion for an 'interim' aircraft pending proper introduction of the Whirlwind. Bristol started building a prototype by taking a part-built Beaufort out of the production line. This conversion would speed the process - Bristol had promised series production in early 1940 on the basis of a order being placed in February 1939 - and the Ministry ordered two prototypes from the line and two built from scratch. Although it had been expected that maximum re-use of Beaufort components would speed the process, the fuselage needed more work than expected and had to be completely redesigned. As such the first prototype flew for the first time on 17 July 1939, a little more than eight months after the design had started, possibly due to the use of much of the Beaufort's design and parts. A production contract for 300 machines 'off the drawing board' had already been placed two weeks before the prototype F.17/39 even flew.

The first Beaufighter achieved 335 mph at 16,800 ft, the second prototype when laden with operational equipment was slower at 309 mph at 15,000 ft. Large orders were placed, but this meant an expected shortage of Hercules engines. In February 1940, conversion of three aircraft to Merlins was ordered; success with the design was expected to lead to production aircraft in 1941. The first Merlin powered aircraft flew in June 1940.

The interior of the Beaufighter fuselage showing the Z-section and box frames, the bulb-angle stringers and the floor built on two longitudinal keels. The legs of the rotating seat for the observer were mounted on the keels.

1941 saw the development of the Beaufighter Mk.IC long-range heavy fighter. This new variant entered service in May 1941 with a detachment from 252 Sqn operating from Malta. The aircraft proved so effective in the Mediterranean against shipping, aircraft and ground targets that Coastal Command became the major user of the Beaufighter.

The Beaufighter arrived at squadrons in Asia and the Pacific in mid-1942. It has been said - although it was originally a piece of RAF whimsy quickly taken up by a British journalist - that Japanese soldiers referred to the Beaufighter as the 'whispering death', because attacking aircraft often were not heard until too late. The Beaufighter's Hercules engines used sleeve valves which lacked the noisy valve gear common to poppet valve engines.

Owing to its twin power plant, heavy armament and radio-location equipment, the cockpit of the Beaufighter had considerably more controls and instruments than most fighter aircraft.

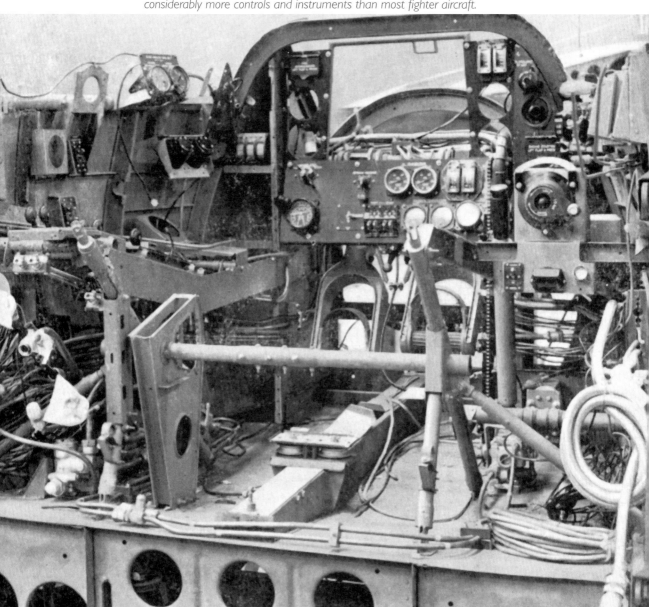

The rear fuselage of the Beaufighter is offered up to the centre section on an adjustable trolley specially designed for the purpose.

The Beaufighter found itself coming off the production line at almost exactly the same time as the first British Airborne Intercept (AI) radar sets. With the four 20 mm cannon mounted in the lower fuselage, the nose could accommodate the radar antennas, and the spaciousness of the fuselage enabled the AI equipment to be fitted easily. Even loaded to 20,000 lb the aircraft was fast enough to catch German bombers. By early 1941, it was an effective counter to Luftwaffe night raids. A night-fighter Mk VIF was supplied to squadrons in March 1942, equipped with AI Mark VIII radar. As the faster De Havilland Mosquito took over in the night fighter role in mid to late 1942, the heavier Beaufighters made valuable contributions in other areas such as anti-shipping, ground attack and interdiction in every operational threatre.

In the Mediterranean, the USAAF received 100 Beaufighters during the summer of 1943, achieving their first victory in July. Through the summer the squadrons conducted both daytime convoy escort and ground-attack operations, but primarily flew defensive interception missions at night.

The stern section of this Beaufighter is offered up to the rear fuselage on its trolley and adjusted by checking the rudder post against a plumb line.

80

The North Coates Strike Wing of Coastal Command, based on the Lincolnshire coast, developed tactics which used large formations of Bristol Beaufighters using cannon and rockets. These tactics were put into practice in mid 1943, and in a 10-month period, 29,762 tons of shipping were sunk. Tactics were further adapted when shipping left port during the night. North Coates Strike Wing operated as the largest anti-shipping force of the Second World War, and accounted for over 150,000 tons of shipping and 117 vessels for a loss of 120 Beaufighters and 241 aircrew killed or missing.

In the South-East Asian Theatre, the Beaufighter Mk VIF operated from India on night missions against Japanese lines of communication in Burma and Thailand. The high-speed, low-level attacks were highly effective, despite often atrocious weather conditions, and makeshift repair and maintenance facilities.

As an aside, Bristol Aircraft seems to have used captial letters to denote their mark numbers - *ie* Mk.VIF - where all other manufactureres used lower case - ie Spitfire Mk. 5c.

The centre section was supported in two cast-iron fixtures by means of eight pin joints during assembly operations.

Before Department of Aircraft Production Beaufighters arrived at Royal Australian Air Force units in the South West Pacific theatre, the Bristol Beaufighter Mk IC was employed in anti-shipping missions.

The most famous of these was the Battle of the Bismarck Sea, where they were used in the fire-suppression role in a mixed force with USAAF A-20 Boston and B-25 Mitchell bombers.

30 Sqn RAAF Beaufighters flew in at mast height to provide heavy suppressive fire for the waves of attacking bombers. The Japanese convoy, under the impression that they were under torpedo attack, made the fatal tactical error of turning their ships towards the Beaufighters, leaving them exposed to skip bombing attacks by the US medium bombers. The Beaufighters inflicted maximum damage on the ships' anti-aircraft guns, bridges and crews during strafing runs with their four 20 mm nose cannons and six wing-mounted .303 in machine guns. Eight transports and four destroyers were sunk for the loss of five aircraft, including one Beaufighter.

A partially-completed Beaufighter sitting in its assembly fixture.

One little known fact about Beaufighter operations is that late 1944, RAF Beaufighter units were engaged in the Greek Civil War, finally withdrawing in 1946.

The Beaufighter was also used by the air forces of Portugal, Turkey and the Dominican Republic. It was used briefly by the Israeli Air Force when some ex RAF examples were clandestinely purchased in 1948.

Many aircraft were converted to the target tug role postwar as the TT.10 and served with several RAF support units until 1960. The last flight of a Beaufighter in RAF service was by TT.10 RD761 from RAF Seletar on 12 May 1960.

The outer wing of this Beaufighter is supported on padded trestles before being bolted into place. They were bolted to the centre section by four pin joints.

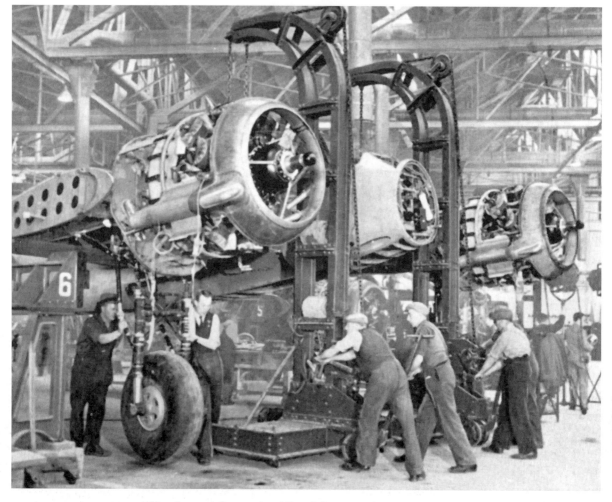

Lifting the partially-completed Beaufighter out of its assembly fixture.

By the time British production lines shut down in September 1945, supposedly some 5,564 Beaufighters had been built in Britain, by Bristol and also by Fairey Aviation Company at Stockport and RAF Ringway (498); Ministry of Aircraft Production (3336) and Rootes at Speke (260). When Australian production ceased in 1946, 365 Mk.21s had been built.

The Beaufighter Mk X with rockets. This machine is NE255/EE-H of No. 404 Squadron RCAF, of RAF Coastal Command at Davidstow Moor, 21 August 1944.

As Director of the Beaufort Division of the Department of Aircraft Production in Australia, John Storey was responsible for the production of Beaufighters there. Mr. Storey joined the Aircraft Production Commission at the request of the Commonwealth Government early in 1940, assuming full control of Beaufort production shortly afterwards, and became a member of the Aircraft Advisory Committee. Here he talks about how it happened.

'Actually the first batch of engineering drawings and technical data for the Beaufighter did not arrive from Bristol until March, 1943, but we were able to put the first Beaufighter into the air on May 26, 1944, and deliver it to the Air Force five days later. This was a creditable achievement for a country like Australia, owing to our limited background of aircraft construction experience, and also because, before the first aircraft came off the assembly line, we were required to incorporate and develop most extensive modifications.   By September we had achieved quantity production, although in the interim we had to convert our plants to Beaufighter production and at the same time finish off our Beaufort programme.

Front fuselages for Beaufighters were built in an annexe to the New South Wales Railways workshops.

Looking down the Beaufighter assembly line at a Beaufort-Division plant. At least one serial visible here is A8-222.

The Beaufighter being built in Australia was the Mark XXI. At the outset, we were required to build it as a torpedo-carrier, but before we had got properly into production the torpedo role was abandoned and we had to turn our attention to equipping the aircraft for other functions. This, with numerous modifications to adapt the Beaufighter to tropical conditions, made the task anything but an easy one. Amongst other changes, we substituted four 0.5 inch Browning guns for the previous six 0.303 guns in the wings, installed a rearward-firing gun and substituted pneumatic cannon-cocking control for manual selection, which permitted better harmonisation. We provided for rockets or bombs under the wings, completely redesigned the electrical and radio installations, repositioned and extensively modified the fuel system, fitted a tailwheel with anti-shimmy device, and made provision for the installation of the Sperry automatic pilot should it be required.

Before we were able to embark on Beaufighter production, we had to deal with some 70,000 negatives of engineering and tooling drawings and technical data, necessitating the establishment of a special photographic unit. Enlargements from these negatives made on semi-transparent linotone or mastertrace paper were used as tracings. Simultaneously, groups of technicians were sent to England to study manufacturing methods and processes at Bristol and elsewhere, and steps were taken to organize the manufacture of parts. In one respect we were in luck, for owing to the generosity of Great Britain we received the Hercules power eggs complete from England'.

MAKING BEST USE OF LABOUR

A interesting scheme for decentralised part-timer workshops was organised by a resident of one of the London suburbs in 1942. The prototype shop, which had been running successfully in the lounge of a large house, employed forty half-time women from the immediate neighbourhood on hand-finishing aircraft components for a hard-pressed factory in Middlesex to which the organiser was introduced by the Regional Board. Further shops for various hand-assembly and non-machine operation soon sprang up with the support of officials of the Ministries of Production and Aircraft Production, as well as various prominent industrialists. It was realized that the scheme was worth taking seriously as it had big potentialities of bringing war work to the enormous reserve of woman-power that still existed in residential districts.

The Ministry of Production, in conjunction with the Ministry of Labour and Supply Departments, extended the plan and by 1943 figures showed that there were some 20,000 outworkers in Britain, many in rural districts, but nearly half of them in the London area. Such was the success, that more work had to be found, as the number of non-mobile women who had volunteered enabled the

Assembling electrical instruments in a former furniture showroom in the London area. There were 33 volunteers in this particular centre.

scheme to be considerably extended, and managements were urged to utilise their labour and so relieve bottlenecks in their own factories. By taking work to workrooms in country and suburban districts the productive capacity of women unable to leave their localities was profitably harnessed to the war effort.

De Havilland's made particular use of this available labour force and 'out-worked' a lot of small components for their Mosquitoes. Obviously, long runs of light parts were the most suitable for outworking. Cable harness, electric terminals, certain types of lamps, wireless parts, armature coils, condensers, and the assembly of small units offered the greatest scope for the scheme. A high degree of skill and accuracy was attained by women producing particular components in their own homes or local workrooms

Mosquito production did not always entail the use of large factories. Mrs B A Hale formed a 'cottage industry' group with her neighbours to make Mosquito parts in a hut in the garden of her Welwyn home - it was a novel kind of 'dispersal of industry' to which many others took part.

A large outworking unit engaged in packing parts at a converted wallpaper factory. Discipline and spirit were up to the best factory standards ; absenteeism was low and lateness almost unknown. Output rate was high, since half-timers could keep up speed on repetitive work and, as they live within walking distance of their work, travelling fatigue and worries were eliminated.

The success of outworking in the London area may be gauged from the following examples, which were typical of centres set up throughout the country. One very large firm of retail house furnishers, with branches throughout the Home Counties, cleared part of three large showrooms and installed the necessary workbenches. Altogether, some 1,100 housewives working in 5-hour shifts were regularly engaged with the preparation of cables for the electrical wiring for a number of different aircraft, and with coil winding for electrical components. This particular scheme was sponsored by the furnishing firm, working in conjunction with the main contractors.

A scheme of a slightly different nature was that carried on at a private house. Here, some 84 friends and acquaintances who lived within easy walking distance were engaged with binding of intercommunication cords in a large room on the ground floor, and up to the end of September 1943 some 14,000 cords had been completed. In addition, another contract for the manufacture of goggles was being completed by individuals in their own homes, the central depot for distribution being organised by the organiser of the above scheme. On this latter work, 70 volunteers were employed. The labour obtained in this case was of a type which was non-directable and immobile and would not come in the jurisdiction of the Ministry of Labour. Another unit was started by a Rotary club, some of whose members had practical knowledge of motor engineering, electrical equipment and assembly. Here a contract was secured for the assembly of gunsight lamp.

In the London and South-Eastern region, 320 National Fire Service station carried out productive work. At first this was of a simple nature, but later increased in skill and included work of somewhat heavier type. Because it was impossible to obtain further local labour, a London firm decided to form outworking centres in residential districts. Soon there were a large number of units in operation and these were completely assembling components made in the main factory.

Factory piecework rates were paid, and up to £2 a week was earned. Overheads were very low, being in the region of fifteen per cent of the actual bench labour costs.

MAKING THE CANNON

One of the most effective replies to the introduction of protective armour plating to enemy aircraft was the equipping of British machines with the highly successful 20 mm. Hispano cannon.

As the name implies, the Hispano cannon was developed by the French company Hispano-Suiza. It was based on the earlier Swiss Oerlikon FF S weapons, which the company manufactured under license in France. Great Britain had acquired a license to build the cannon, which was first used in a British fighter as the Hispano Mk.I with the Westland Whirlwind of 1940. British engineers developed a belt-feeding mechanism.

Four cannon replaced the eight Browning .303 machine guns in the Hurricane Mk. IIc and in Spitfire Mk. Vc, and became standard armament in late-war British fighters such as the Typhoon/Tempest family or late marks of the Spitfire. Although earlier Spitfires equipped with Type C wing could accomodate four cannon, most carried only two because of technical difficulties such as inadequate gun-heating capacity for the outboard cannon leading to the gun freezing at high altitiudes.

The manufacturing requirements of this cannon called for a very high standard of accuracy and surface finish. In spite of such complications as hard material and difficult shapes, factors which considerably curtailed the adoption of true quantity production methods, these requirements were maintained with semi-skilled and female operatives. Very little special-purpose equipment was used, but there was an extensive employment of standard machine tools fitted with suitable fixtures.

A Churchill - Conomatic multi-spindle lathe set up for the production of Hispano firing pins. As with many production facilities during wartime, the machine is in the charge of a female operator.

Above left: early machining operations on the barrel exterior. Observe the cams fitted to this Fay automatic to reproduce the tapers. Above right: a Newall thread grinder specially modified for grinding from solid metal the breech thread on the barrel.

This gun was notable in that it possessed a mechanically locked breech block when firing with either single shots or automatic fire. Initial forward movement of the breech block mechanism was obtained from a return spring. With the breech block in its most forward position the cartridge was slightly crushed in the barrel chamber, and the locking mechanism prevented any rearward movement of the breech block. The firing pin was then allowed to come forward, striking the cap.

Unlocking was performed by gas pressure from the barrel, and residual pressure in the chamber forced the breech block rearwards, effecting extraction of the cartridge case and introducing a or as long as the trigger was depressed. In single fire, after each shot the breech was maintained in the cocked position, and no new cartridge was introduced into the chamber.

A very high standard of dimensional accuracy and surface finish was essential to ensure interchangeability of parts and accurate working of the various sliding members at high speeds and pressures. The attainment and maintenance of these ideals was complicated by the hard, tough nature of the materials used.

Boring through the barrel of a Hispano cannon with a six-foot long, hollow D-form tool. Pressurised coolant was passed through the centre of the tool to the cutting edge, which then flushed out the metal swarf. Behind the machine were stacked rows of barrel blanks awaiting machining.

A special purpose American LeBlond lathe for rifling the Hispano barrel. The tool cut on the return stroke and was rotated by a spiral guide.

In spite of these production difficulties, the necessary results were achieved with an average of only ten per cent. skilled labour. Approximately half the operatives making Hispano cannon components in the UK were women, and the equipment under their care included such machines as Churchill-Conomatics multi-spindle lathes, LeBlond deep-hole boring, rifling and lapping machines and other machine tools of an equally complicated nature.

By skilful planning all machining operations were split up into their most elementary form, and extensive use was made of simple holding fixtures which incorporate foolproof location. Much of the grinding is done with the aid of magnetic chucks. By these means, average final milling tolerances of +/- 0·05 mm. (+/-0.002in.) and grinding limits of +/-0.025 mm. were ensured.

Very few special-purpose machines were used, most of the equipment being of standard design. In spite of the toughness of the materials, milling speeds of 50 ft./min. and feeds of 3-4 in./min. were maintained by the use of coarse-tooth, high-power roller mills with a 30, 45 or 60 degree, quick spiral teeth. Practically all lathe operations were performed with single-point Wimet tools.

Lapping the rifling and bore on a LeBlond lathe - for the former operation a new lap was cast in lead inside each barrel to ensure accurate fitting.

The R. K. LeBlond Machine Tool Company in Cincinnati, Ohio, was a well known manufacturer of machinist lathes and provided many machines for UK aircraft manufacture.

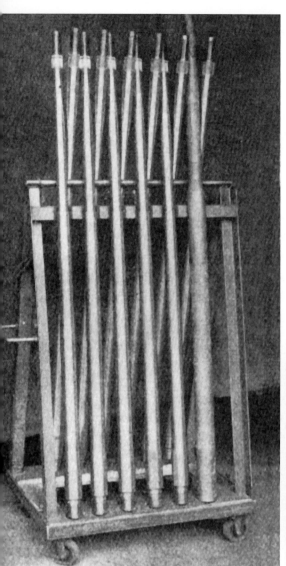

Great care and consideration was given to every aspect of jig and tool design for the Hispano cannon in that every aspect to production was broken down to it's most simple form and then making use of specific fixtures, jigs and cutting devices to allow the performance of individual operations by unskilled or semi-skilled operators.

Likewise the inspection of components was considerably facilitated by the provision of simple, foolproof gauging fixtures whch could be handled safely by unskilled workers.

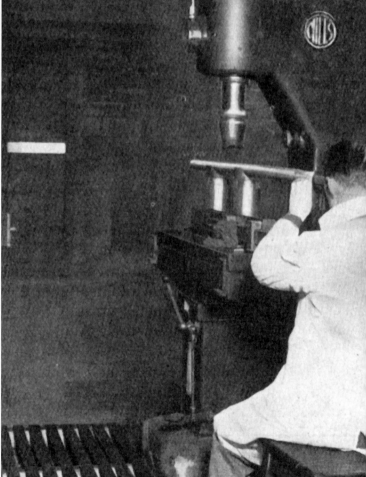

Right: the inspection of a Hisano barrel for straightness was done by viewing a strip of light through the bore, which produced a series of differering shadow forms down the bore, dependant on how far the barrel was out of line.

The inspector could then use the hydraulic press on which the barrel was resting to make any corrections until the barrel was within acceptable tolerance of straightness.

THE WOODEN WONDER

Authorititvely described in 1943 as the fastest operational aircraft in the world, the de Havilland Mosquito was the first modern first-line machine of all-wood construction to go into service. It was a twin-engined mid-wing cantilever monoplane built in two basic versions - bomber and fighter. Of these two there were many sub-variants, including day and night bomber and intruder types.

Structurally, the most outstanding feature of the aircraft was the fuselage built on the balsa-plywood sandwich principle introduced by the de Havilland Company prior to the war and first used in the four-engine Albatross civil transport. The power plant consisted of two Rolls-Royce Merlin engines.

Armament of the Mosquito fighter was a combination of four 20mm Hispano cannon and four Browning .303 machine guns, although as with everything about the Mosquito, a number of variations were possible, including the replacement of the 20mm cannon for a single 57mm gun with just two Brownings for sighting purposes!

Mk XVI Mosquito converted to carry H2X radar for the US 8th Air Force with additional slipper fuel tanks under the wings.

The first stage of fuselage half-shell assembly saw the bulkheads and other members of the internal structure located in slots in the mould.

Stage two saw the inner skin and between skin structure put into place.

Stage three of Mosquito fuselage construction was the fitment of balsa-wood fillers that formed the central portion of the sandwich.

After the outer shell was fitted into place, this was then covered with flexible steel bands under tension in order to provide the required pressure for bonding all the glued elements together.

Equipment was installed inside the two half fuselage sections prior to boxing up. In this case it is a bomber variant being built, but the process was the same for both fighters and bombers. The trunnion mounting for the wing attachment pick-ups is seen in the centre of the two halves.

The rear floor was fitted, rudder and elevator-operating linkage mounted in the cockpit floor and a start was made with the electrical wiring, and with the plumbing of the oxygen and hydraulic systems.

A point of interest in Mosquito fuselage construction was the simplification of assembly by arranging the control cable runs down the port side of the fuselage and the hydraulic plumbing as far as possible along the starboard side. The control column was also mounted on the port half-shell and connected to the rudder and elevator linkage before the joining stage was reached.

Above: This view, from the tail end of the fuselage shows the boxing up fixture that brings the two half-shells together. The series of five circular clamps holding the two halves together were in fact each made from two laminated timber halves held together and thereby applying pressure by adjustable turnbuckles.

Right: The leveling and drilling jigs in place for drilling the No. 6 bulkhead for the fin front pick-ups.

Above: the bottom rear spar boom laminations in the cementing fixture.

The Mosquito wing was very distinctive. It was made in one piece from tip to tip and was based on conventional two-spar practice with the usual interspar rib structure. The stressed-skin covering, however, was a departure from the usual type of construction. The birch plywood skin was reinforced by closely-spaced, square-section, spanwise stringers of Douglas fir, which, over the upper surface of the wing were sandwiched between a double covering of skin. On the under surface, the outboard panels of the skin were of identical construction but with only one skin. Over the centre portion of the span, where the fuel tanks were housed between the spars, the wing under surface was completed by stressed covers to the tank bays. These tank doors were of balsa-plywood sandwich construction, with bolting edges of shear resistant material.

Below left: Rough machining a bottom boom on an overhead planer. Below right: Spindling lightening recesses in a top spar-boom extension.

The main fixtures for rear-spar assembly. For applying the skin to the forward face of the spar the inverted fixture in the foreground was used.

Assembly of the spars was done in large fixtures with sloped access platforms made necessary by the swept-forward outboard ends of the spars. The booms were very simply located between blocks on the base of the fixture at each side. Longitudinal locationwas given by the combined forward sweep and dihedral in conjunction with a chordwise taper on the top and bottom faces of the boom. A slight excess length was left on the tips of the booms and was trimmed off in the fixture. It is worthy of note that a tolerance of 0.020 inches was maintained on the overall length of each half of the boom.

The booms were secured in the fixture by wedges driven in against their inner faces and the locating blocks. Spruce spacing members between the booms were positioned on the fixture to templates located over the faces of the booms. Beetle cement - a form of Urea-Formaldehyde Resin glue - was applied to the booms and spacers and to the underside of the web, which was then laid in position and screwed down, the screws providing the pressure required for the bonding of the joint. Owing to the increased setting time required for this cement as compared with the adhesive formerly used, and the fact that no other work could be done on the spar during the setting period, it became necessary to devise a means of accelerating the setting of the cement in order to avoid creating a bottleneck at this stage.

It was well known that the setting of synthetic adhesives could be speeded up by raising their temperature and it was decided to make use of this fact and to adopt some form of electrical heating. The problem was not a simple one, as direct application of heat to the cement line was not possible and the area to be considered varied considerably across the span of the spar. The problem was solved by the application of wooden panels with heating elements embedded in their lower faces.

The complete drilling jig for the rear spar.

From the inverted fixture, the spars were transferred to the drilling jig, in which the holes were drilled for all the metal fittings that were mounted on the spar, such as the undercarriage and the hinge brackets for the ailerons on the rear face.

Bush plates were provided for drilling from both faces of the spar, which was supported and located between each pair of wooden pads below and on each side. The bottom pad could be raised or lowered by screw adjustment to set the height of the spar in the jig and the pads on one side of the fixture could be screwed in to clamp the spar in position. Setting was made to a longitudinal datum line and a vertical datum at the centre line, both of which were laid out on the spar web from templates in the main assembly fixture. The longitudinal datum was set to pointers mounted on the jig base.

Colour coding was used to distinguish the bushes for different drill diameters and a portable drill was used. The production of these large components in wood to a tolerance of ± 0.040 inches over a length of 50 feet was an achievement which reflected the greatest credit upon the sub-contractors.

A close-up view of the centre drill plates and locations on the spar-drilling jig for the rear spar.

An early stage of assembly in the wing fixture. Both spars were in position and most of the ribs have been fitted between them.

In a separate area skin panels were bring drilled from wooden templates, as seen in the left of this picture. In the centre, stringers have been laid out in the slots of the asssembly fixture while on the right, ply skin is being applied over a similar set. Cement was applied to the top faces of the stringers and the underside of the skin which was then laid over the stringers, located against metal stops from the edge of the tables and screwed down by pump-action screwdrivers. The screws provided the required pressure to make the joint, thus forming the inner surface of the wing skin.

Above: the inner shell in position. The centre section stringer scarf joints have been fitted and the wooden wedge cramps were in place to hold them during the setting of the cement.

Left: a close-up of the centre section of the inner shell, showing the wooden wedge cramps in place on the stringers.

Left: drilling the walnut panels for the attachment of the forward fuselage pick-ups on the upper wing surface.

Applying the upper surface skin to the wing.

The wing assembly shop - fitting and installation work is proceeding in the foreground.

Engine and radiator fairings were fitted to the top wing surface and the aileron and flap-control cables were assembled, but not connected up. For transport to the doping shop, the wing was slung on the overhead crane in the vertical position and mounted on two bogies which picked-up on the engine fittings. The usual red dope, madapolam covering and camouflage were applied in the dope shop, from which the wing emerged into the installation section. One small doping operation on the back of the shroud was done off the bogies as access could not be obtained to it in the shop.

Installation of electrical and hydraulic services was then completed and the engine support struts assembled. Tanks were also installed. The wing was then ready for transport to final assembly.

Doping a completed wing. All the lamps in the dope shop were shielded by glass from the dope fumes. The wings were transported from the assembly shop on wheeled bogies.

Above: Mosquito wings passing through the final stages of equipment installation before despatch to the final assembly area. The flaps and ailerons were already in position, but the wing-tips were yet to be installed.

Right: The assembly fixture for the Mosquito wing-tip, the edges of which were made from multiple laminations. For attachment to the wing a Bakelite-reinforced strip was fitted to the inboard edges and screws inserted through to a series of anchor-nuts around the inside of a corresponding flange on the wing.

Setting up for drilling the strap plate and radius rod fittings on the Mosquito undercarriage leg.

The building of the undercarriage leg was a matter of straightforward assembly. As received from the press-shop, the joint flanges and ends of the half-casings were pierced ready for assembly, which commenced with the temporary joining of a pair of pressings by the insertion of service bolts or rivets through the flanges.

Right: a close-up of the jig showing the clamping and bushings for drilling the radius rod fittings on a radial drill.

Riveting the two halves together was then completed on a bench-mounted squeeze-riveting machine.

As small variations in form were almost inevitable on an assembly built up in this way from pressings, a sizing operation was carried out on the interior of the completed casing. This operation, performed on a horizontal broaching machine, was rather burnishing than broaching, as metal was not actually removed from the interior of the casing.

Sizing the internal form of the undercarriage leg casing. This was performed on a horizontal broaching machine by pulling a die of the correct shape and size through it.

Left: The piston tube, piston, rebound rubber and guide block assembly of a Mosquito undercarriage leg.

Right: the complete leg assembly with external casing.

Below left: Inserting the leg assembly into the casing. The pack of rubber blocks and their associated spacers were temporarily held in place by an assembly rod that was removed though the top cap after final assembly.

Bottom right: screwing the casing to the guide-block with the rubbers held under compression in a screw press.

The first stage of tailplane assembly - front spars, nose ribs and leading edges were built up as a separate unit.

Assembly of the tailplane was done in two stages in vertical fixtures. The front spar had already been drilled and the fuselage pick-up fittings were first assembled to the existing holes. The spar was located to datum centre lines on the front web. Locations were also provided on the fixture for the outboard end ribs, to control the overall length. This was important, as the horn balances of the elevators overlapped the tips of the tailplane and proper clearance for their working was essential.

Rib posts were already in position on the spar faces and the nose ribs were positioned from them and from slot locations formed by two sections of angle iron mounted on the fixture. The spar was supported from beneath at several points. Alignment of datum centre lines on ribs and spar determined the final setting of the ribs and leading edge bend were then cemented and pinned in position. Final shaping of this edge and fairing in of the rib profiles was done by hand on the fixture, templates being used to check the profile at each rib station. As with the front spar, the fittings were first mounted on the rear spar out of the fixture. The centre hinge fittings, incorporating the elevator trimming adjustment, was mounted, followed by the outer tailplane hinge brackets.

In the main assembly fixture, the rear spar was located on these hinge fittings, while the leading-edge was located from the fuselage attachment fittings on the front spar. Box-type interspar ribs were assembled by sliding them in over the rib posts mounted on the inner web of each spar and gluing and pinning them in place. Fairing of the rib profiles was completed by hand shaping.

The skin - complete with handholds, inspection hatches and strengthening - was applied by Beetle cement and was also screwed and pinned to the structure.

In the main tailplane assembly fixture, the rear spar, leading edge and interspar ribs were brought together to make the complete unit.

Some later marks of Mosquito carried wing mounted overload or 'slipper' fuel tanks. Very little has ever appeared in print about these devices, indeed, many do not realise that they were moulded out of plywood veneers. This type of moulding represents probably the first application of this production technique to the manufacture of plywood units of compound curvature in the UK.

For ease of moulding, the Mosquito tank was divided into nose and tail sections, the joint being made roughly midway in its length. Two similar half-mouldings were made at each pressing in the autoclave. The inside jacket was first placed in position and to give stability to the whole assembly was stapled around its open edges to the mould. The other two were then dropped over it, followed by a rubber bag. A clamping frame was lowered over the rubber to secure it to the platform, and create an airtight joint.

Initial atmospheric pressure on the mould was then obtained by pumping out the air from beneath the rubber bag, after which the mould on its mobile platform was pushed into the autoclave. Steam and compressed air were used together to give the necessary heat and pressure. While the moulds were in the autoclave another two were being prepared on a track outside. There were several variants of this process, among which were Duramold, Vidal and Timm. In the Duramould process a female mould was used and in the Timm and Vidal methods a male former.

The scarf joint between the forward and aft sections of the tank was bonded under the pressure maintained by a series of screw jacks.

Top: drilling the tank shell for the internal structure from a basket-type jig.

Middle: the first stage of assembling the internal structure: applying adhesive to the bulkhead baffles.

Bottom: the inner bulkhead baffles were secured to the shell by countersunk screws as well as adhesive.

A reinforcing structure was fitted inside the nose half of the tank, consisting of a small laminated bulkhead or frame with two stringers or longerons. This structure was made up as a separate unit before being both glued and screwed to the tank shell.

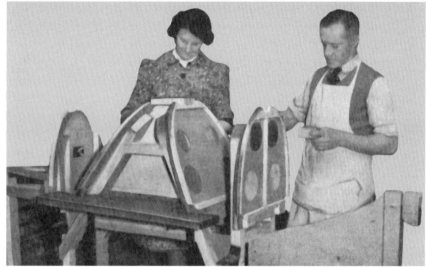

It was at this stage that the panel which formed the upper portion of the nose was assembled. For this operation the nose section of the tank was located in a wooden fixture. Adhesive was applied to the nose reinforcing structure and this also was inserted into the nose shell.

When it was in its correct position, the two stringers were centrally disposed over the joints between the separate panel and the main nose section. With the panel in position the plywood was marked out drilled, then screwed and glued into position before trimming.

To seal the screw holes and to make the tank completely fuel-proof, the interior was subjected to a sloshing treatment. In order to cover the whole of the interior the tank was held in two rotatable cradles (left) which were carried in a frame.

This permitted the tilting of the tank to any angle. A sequence of positions was followed with two cycles of operation - a slow slosh and a quick slosh.

In the slow slosh, the tank was left for five minutes in each position, in the quick slosh it was moved continuously from one position to the next. An ICI zinc-chromate compound was used, about 20 gallons being placed in the tank, after which the air pressure was pumped up to 1 lb./sq. in. for the first slush and to 2 lb./sq. in for the second one.

After the sloshing operation the tank was placed in a drying chamber where a stream of air was passed through the fuel pipe into the interior and out through the filler hole. Drying requires a period of four hours, during which excess compound was also drained from the tank.

A pressure test for leaks was next performed (right) on the tanks, air being pumped in to a pressure of 2.25lb. /sq. in., which had to be maintained for a period of twenty minutes without falling below 2 .lb./sq. in. The tanks were then covered in madapolam and doped, after which the pressure test was repeated.

ALL WIRED UP

Some time before the outbreak of World War Two serious consideration was given to the fact that aircraft electrical wiring might create serious bottlenecks in production, unless a system could be evolved to make it possible to pre-assemble a simple, complete wiring-harness in widely-dispersed factories. It was also felt that simplicity, lightness and ease of maintenance in service under war conditions would be factors of primary importance.

The pre-war practice of working to a wiring diagram and wiring each aircraft separately was both undesirable and impracticable for wartime methods of manufacture under dispersal conditions. With these and a number of other major considerations in mind, a wiring system of the 'open wiring' type was evolved and tested by Vickers-Armstrongs (Supermarine) Ltd., with the co-operation of Joseph Lucas Ltd. The pins required for this type of work of special moulded-plastic material for lightness and non-conducting, were developed by Oddie, Bradbury and Cull Ltd.

The tests proved to be so successful that it was decided to adopt this form of wiring for production, and its advantages have proved themselves in service over a long period, under extreme conditions. This system was based upon the use of single-core cables, bunched in looms, over which were passed short lengths of poly-vinyl-chloride sleeves. A hole was punched in the PVC sleeve, to take the special pins which, in turn, were pushed through the cables. The harness, or loom, was attached to the airframe by the Oddie pins which engaged in special clips riveted to the airframe structure. The ends of the separate cables engaged in their appropriate connectors.

A resilient washer was fitted under the head of the pin on the original installation, so that should it be found necessary to introduce additional cables on later modifications, this washer could be removed and the original pin used on the increased thickness of the loom.

Workers assembling looms on jig-boards which were inclined at an angle for greater convienience in wiring and at a height to eliminate unnecessary effort.

For the first stage the cables were cut off to the correct lengths. This operation was done on simple jigs, the cable being fed automatically, and guillotined. The cable lengths were then stripped on a special electrically heated device, which ensured that the stripping was carried out without damage to the conductors. Next, the cable lengths were fitted with their appropriate connectors, terminals or eyelets. There were a number of ingenious but simple machines which perform these operations.

Identification of the cables was the next step and was carried out by lettered and numbered adhesive tape, specially developed for this wiring system, and produced by Cable Assemblies Ltd., a subsidiary of Herts Pharmaceuticals, Ltd. Completed cable lengths were then grouped in racks in their appropriate lengths in readiness for forming the looms.

The PVC sleeves, approximately one to two inches in length, and of various diameters, were usually manufactured by Tenaplas Ltd., They were cut to length in a single process on a simple press from continuous tube, the hole for the pins punched, and the lines indicating the locked position of the pins marked.

A close-up of one of the completed looms on the assembly jig board.

FIGHTERS TO TRAIN - THE MILES MASTER

Shapely Miles Masters (Rolls-Royce Kestrel XXX engine) of wood construction are now passing into service in numbers which will increase week by week for some time to come. This advanced trainer has a high performance and carries practically all the equipment which is to be found on a modern military aircraft, including a machine gun and a camera gun. The machines are seen on the assembly line at the works of Phillips and Powis Aircraft Ltd. Reading.

If it was not for training aircraft, there would be no fighters. One advanced trainer that provided a good stepping stone between primary trainers such as the DH82 Tiger Moth and front line fighters was the Miles Master.

The original company was founded by Charles Powis and Jack Phillips as Philips and Powis Aircraft after meeting Fred Miles. The company was based on Woodley Aerodrome in Woodley, near the town of Reading and in the county of Berkshire.

Miles was the name used to market the aircraft of British engineer Frederick George Miles, who designed numerous light civil and military aircraft and a range of curious prototypes. The name 'Miles' was associated with two distinct companies that Miles was involved in and was also attached to several designs produced before there was a company trading under Miles' name.

In 1936 Rolls-Royce bought into the company and although aircraft were produced under the Miles name, it was not until 1943 that the firm became Miles Aircraft Limited when Rolls-Royce's interests were bought out.

Above: the Miles Master wing centre-section department

Below: the fuselage assembly section, showing the eight cantilever fuselage jigs which were arranged in four pairs.

The M.9A Master I was based on the M.9 Kestrel trainer that was first demonstrated at the Hendon Air Show in July 1937, although it never entered production. The production Master I, which first flew on 31 March 1939, used the lower-powered 715 hp Rolls-Royce Kestrel XXX engine, reducing the maximum speed. Nonetheless it remained one of the fastest and most manoeuvrable trainers of its day, and possibly one of the most asthetically pleasing! The Master entered service just before the start of the war and eventually 900 Mk. I and Mk. Ia Masters were built. This total included 26 built as the M.24 Master Fighter which were modified to a single-seat configuration, and armed with six .303 in machine guns for use as an emergency fighter, but did not see combat.

Fuselages left the fuselage assembly bay and were then fitted with instrument panels and other equipment before being passed to the main assembly lines.

Left: Miles Master Instrument panels were among the units which were almost completely assembled on the bench.

Below: Stage II on the main assembly line. Hydraulic lines for the undercarriage were being connected up and the machine was about to be lowered on to its own wheels

The later stage in the general assembly. The engine has been mounted in position, and the radiators, ready for attachment, may be seen lying beneath the fuselage.

When production of the Kestrel engine ceased, a new variant of the Master was designed to use the 870 hp air-cooled radial Bristol Mercury XX engine. The first M.19 Master II prototype flew on 30 October 1939 and 1,748 were eventually built. When the Lend-Lease programme began to supply engines from the United States, a third variant of the Master, the M.27 Master III was designed, powered by the American 825 hp Pratt & Whitney Twin Wasp Junior two-row radial engine. A total of 602 Master IIIs were built before production of the Miles Martinet took over in 1942.

As Don Brown who worked for Miles recalls, things got rather chaotic: *'During 1938 the Air Ministry asked us to consider the substitution of the Bristol Mercury engine for the Rolls-Royce Kestrel engine in the Master, as the latter engine was no longer in production and existing stocks were rapidly becoming depleted. The Bristol Mercury engine, on the other hand, was in large scale production for use in the Blenheim and the Ministry assured us that there would be ample stocks available. The design staff got down to the job and in 1939 the M.19 appeared and was known as the Master II. After preliminary handling trials by our test pilots the machine went for its official service trials in November.*

As was to be expected it passed them. Then the Ministry suddenly found that there were not large stocks of the Mercury engine available after all and promptly asked us to consider the installation of yet another type of engine, this time an American but unfortunately no sooner had we done so than the Ministry discovered that they had got lots of Mercury engines and so the Master II went into production after all. We can only assume that they must have temporarily mislaid them somewhere !

With Master production under way, an imposing new dope shop that was divided into bays by movable metal partitions was constructed at Woodley. In the background on the right was the wood kiln used for drying timber to the correct moisture content.

In trainer form, the Master was equipped to carry eight practice bombs, plus one .303 in Vickers machine gun mounted in the front fuselage. In 1942, all variants had their wings clipped by three feet (one metre) to reduce stress on the wings and increase manoeuvrability. All of the 3,227 Masters produced were built by Phillips and Powis Aircraft Limited at Woodley, Berkshire, the largest number produced of any Miles aircraft type.

Service use primarily revolved around (Pilot) Advanced Flying Units, while several hundred Miles Master IIs were converted, or delivered new, for the glider-towing role, with the bottom of the rudder cut away to allow fitting of a towing hook. Miles Masters were extensively used from 1942 as tugs for Hotspur gliders at Glider Training Schools. Known deployments were to 287 Squadron RAF between February and August 1942 and to 286 Squadron RAF from November 1944 to February 1945.

Left: the two seat tandem cockpit of a Miles Master I - the overall layout did not vary much across of number of Miles' designs.

Below: A Miles Master I in flight

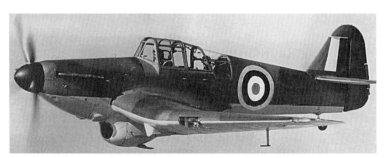

ALAS POOR WALRUS

By the outbreak of the war the Supermarine Walrus - a British single-engine amphibious biplane reconnaissance aircraft designed by R. J. Mitchell and operated by the Fleet Air Arm was already something of an anachronism.

Nevertheless, this single-engined biplane amphibian was a welcome sight for many a downed fighter pilot bobbing around in the English Channel or the North Sea. It was the first British squadron-service aircraft to incorporate a fully retractable main undercarriage, completely enclosed crew accommodation, and an all-metal fuselage.

Left: the Walrus hull was constructed around a central keel inside a form slung from an overhead beam. Bulkheads were then put in place.

Below: Walrus K5552 about to get airborne

Supermarine Walrus frame No. 8, located at the wing forward spar and undercarriage connections as received from a sub-contractor. In many respects this frame was the main strength of the aircraft linking undercarriage, wings and keel together.

As the Walrus was stressed to a level suitable for catapult-launching, rather surprisingly for such an ungainly-looking machine, it could be looped and bunted. This was first done by the test pilot Joseph 'Mutt' Summers, flying the prototype at the SBAC show at Hendon in June 1933; this feat surprised even R. J. Mitchell, who was amongst the spectators. However, in practice any water in the bilges would make its presence felt when the aircraft was inverted. This usually discouraged the pilot from any future aerobatics on this type!

In 1934 an early pre-production Walrus became the first amphibian according to its manufacture to be launched from a land-based catapult. The strength of the aircraft was again demonstrated in 1935, when the prototype was attached to the battleship HMS Nelson at Gibraltar. With the naval commander-in-chief on board the pilot attempted a water touch-down, but with the undercarriage accidentally lowered. The Walrus was immediately flipped over but the occupants only had minor injuries; the machine was later repaired and returned to flight. Soon afterwards, the Walrus became one of the first aircraft to be fitted with an undercarriage position indicator on the instrument panel.

Part of the wing assembly shop. In the foreground was a port upper wing with the fuel tank anchorage jig in position. Beyond it was a reversed port lower wing with the wooden wheel casing fitted.

Angle steel ribbons were employed to space and align the frames positively in position before the skin was applied to the Walrus hull.

By the start of World War Two the Walrus was in widespread use. Although its principal intended use was gunnery spotting in naval actions, this only occurred twice: Walruses from HMS *Renown* and HMS *Manchester* were launched in the Battle of Cape Spartivento and a Walrus from HMS *Gloucester* was used in the Battle of Cape Matapan. The main task of ship-based aircraft was patrolling for Axis submarines and surface-raiders, and by March 1941, Walruses were being deployed with Air to Surface Vessel (ASV) radars to assist in this. During the Norwegian Campaign and the East African Campaign, they also saw very limited use in bombing and strafing shore targets.

By 1943, catapult-launched aircraft on cruisers and battleships were being phased out; their role at sea was taken over by radar. Also, a hangar and catapult occupied a considerable amount of valuable space on a warship. However, Walruses continued to fly from carriers for air-sea rescue and general communications tasks. Their low landing speed meant they could make a carrier landing despite having no flaps or tailhook.

This view shows a lower wing with the aileron jig mounted on the rear spar. On the left can be seen a wheel-casing sub-assembly resting on a wing.

When flying from a warship, the Walrus would be recovered by touching-down alongside, then lifted from the sea by a ship's crane. The aircraft's lifting-gear was kept in a compartment in the section of wing directly above the engine – one of the Walrus' crew would climb onto the top wing and attach this to the crane hook. This was a straightforward procedure in calm waters, but could be very difficult if the conditions were rough. One procedure was for the parent ship to slew several degrees just before the aircraft touched down, thus creating an evanescent 'smooth' astern of the ship on which the Walrus could alight, this being followed by a fast taxi up to the ship before the 'smooth' dissipated.

The RAF used Walruses mainly in the Air-Sea-Rescue role. The specialist air-sea rescue squadrons flew a variety of aircraft, using Spitfires and Boulton Paul Defiants to patrol looking for downed aircrew. Avro Ansons were then used to drop supplies and dinghies, and if required, Walruses were used to pick up aircrew from the water. A number of RAF air-sea rescue squadrons were deployed to cover the waters around the United Kingdom, the Mediterranean Sea and the Bay of Bengal.

Three Walruses, delivered in March 1939, were used by Irish Air Corps as maritime patrol aircraft during the Irish Emergency of World War Two.

After the war, some Walruses continued to see limited military use with the RAF and foreign navies. Eight were operated by Argentina, two flew of which from the cruiser ARA *La Argentina* as late as 1958. Other aircraft were used for training by the French Navy's Aviation Navale.

CONTINUOUS CUTTING BY COPY

The routing portion of a pantograph routing and drilling machine operating on a stack of sheet-metal blanks. Two operatives were required, the one shown on the left guiding the stylus round the templates. In the background can be seen one of the drilling machines which were of similar construction.

For the shaping and drilling of light-alloy sheet metal blanks to a regular consistency, a number of aircraft manufacturers used continuously operating pantograph machines. The complete equipment consisted of a router with two drilling machines and was arranged to work over two parallel tables nearly sixty feet in length. A drilling machine was placed at each end of the tables. Between the tables was a centre rail on which the pantograph unit traversed longitudinally on steel rollers and there were steadying rails at the sides of the tables to prevent the unit from tipping unduly. Rollers were fitted at the extremities of the pantograph to contact the side rails.

The pantograph itself comprised of two carriages superimposed upon one another. Movement of the lower carriage was along the tables on the centre rail, while the upper carriage, which carried the routing stylus and cutter spindle, had transverse movement on slides on the lower carriage. This double right-angled movement was combined to follow the shape of any routing template. A similar arrangement was adopted for the drills located at each end of the tables. The process not only allowed continuous operation, it also created consistant accuracy for a template of known form and dimensions was being followed.

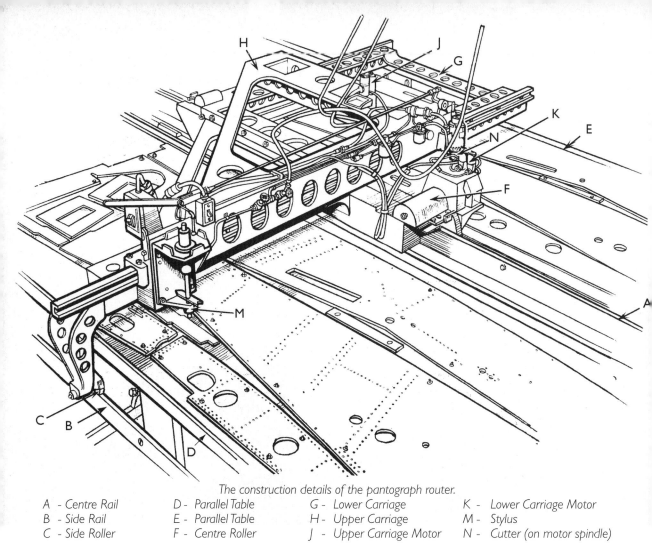

The construction details of the pantograph router.

A - Centre Rail	D - Parallel Table	G - Lower Carriage	K - Lower Carriage Motor
B - Side Rail	E - Parallel Table	H - Upper Carriage	M - Stylus
C - Side Roller	F - Centre Roller	J - Upper Carriage Motor	N - Cutter (on motor spindle)

Power traverse to the longitudinal movement of the lower carriage was provided by four motors. Two of these gave left or forward traverse and two right-hand or reverse movement. The motors were controlled by the operator until the stylus made contact with the template, after which the direction of motion and the cutting speed were controlled by hand pressure between the stylus and template.

Drilling and routing templates were mounted on sheets of plywood and secured to one of the tables. Sheet metal blanks were stacked on the other table opposite and when the first few holes have been drilled were pinned in position. The remaining holes were then drilled, after which the profile was routed to shape.

While one stack of blanks was being drilled and routed, templates and blanks were being placed in position at another position along the tables. The second drill was brought into action on these as soon as the first set of blanks had been machined to shape and the routing head was brought along to complete these in turn. In the meantime the second batch had been drilled at the first station, or still another set at a third station, so that work on the machine could continue without pause. Sliding overhead rails carried electric and compressed air supply lines to the machine.

TOO LATE TO SEE WAR SERVICE - THE DH HORNET

The final assembly shop at Hatfield. The machine on the assembly line has PX236 roughly chalked on the rear fuselage. The aircraft went to serve with 64 Sqn.

The De Havilland Hornet was designed as a private venture for a long-range fighter destined for the Pacific Theatre in the war against Japan, Specification F.12/43 was written around the type. From an early stage it was also envisaged that the Hornet could be adapted for naval use, operating from aircraft carriers. As a result priority was given to ease of control, especially at low speeds, and good pilot visibility. Construction was of mixed balsa/plywood similar to the Mosquito, but the Hornet differed in incorporating stressed Alclad lower-wing skins bonded to the wooden upper wing structure using the then-new adhesive Redux. The two wing spars were redesigned to withstand a higher safety factor of 10 versus 8.

The Hornet prototype RR915 first flew on 28 July 1944 with Geoffrey de Havilland Jr. at the controls. Powered by a pair of R-R Merlin engines, it was the fastest piston-engined fighter in Royal Air Force service. The Hornet also had the distinction of being the fastest wooden aircraft ever built and the second fastest operational twin propeller-driven aircraft — being slightly slower than the unconventional German Dornier Do 335 of 1945. The prototype achieved 485 mph in level flight, which came down to 472 mph in production aircraft.

One of the main wing assembly fixtures showing the two spars and interspar ribs in position. The similarity to the Mosquito wing is noticable.

The DH.103 Hornet further exploited the wooden construction techniques pioneered by de Havilland's classic Mosquito. Entering service at the end of the Second World War, the Hornet equipped postwar RAF Fighter Command day fighter units in the UK and was later used successfully as a strike fighter in Malaya. The Sea Hornet was a carrier-capable version.

It entered service in 1946 with 64 Squadron based at RAF Horsham St Faith in Norfolk. Next to convert to the Hornet was 19 Squadron at RAF Wittering, followed by 41 Squadron and 65 Squadron, both based at RAF Church Fenton. 65 Sqn was to participate in one of the first official overseas visits by an RAF unit when they visited Sweden in May 1948. Pilot conversion to the Hornet was provided by 226 Operational Conversion Unit.

Apart from the revised structure, the Hornet's wings were a synthesis of aerodynamic knowledge gathered since the Mosquito's design process, being much thinner in cross section, with de Havilland designers adopting a laminar flow profile similar to the P-51 Mustang and Hawker Tempest. The control surfaces consisted of hydraulically operated split flaps extending from the wing root to outboard of the engine nacelles; as in the Mosquito, the rear of the nacelles were part of the flap structure. Outboard, the Alclad-covered ailerons extended close to the clipped wing tips and provided excellent roll control.

Fitting the between-the-skin members to the inner skin in the second stage of fuselage assembly. Note the large cut-out for the cockput glazing.

Left: using a jig to drill the fuselage for the wing attachment fittings.

The Hornet used 'slimline' Rolls-Royce Merlin engines that were versions with engine ancillaries repositioned to achieve a minimum frontal area and less drag. The aircraft was somewhat unusual for a British design in that it had propellers that rotated in opposite directions. To achieve this, the engines used slightly different gearboxes, hence the double Merlin marks of 130/131. This feature effectively cancelled out the variable and cumulative torque effect of two propellers turning in the same direction that had affected earlier designs such as the Mosquito. It also reduced the amount of adverse yaw caused by aileron trim corrections and generally provided more stable and predictable behaviour in flight. Initially, the propellers were 'handed' to rotate inboard, rising towards the fuselage, but this was found to reduce the effectiveness of the rudder so propellers rotating outboard were used instead.

Because of the revised induction arrangements of the Merlin 130 series, the supercharger and carburettor air intakes could be placed in the leading edges of the wings, outboard of the nacelles. Other versions of the Merlin, which used 'updraft' induction arrangements, required that the intakes be placed in a duct below the main engine cowling. The main radiators were also mounted in the inboard leading edges of the wings. Internal fuel, to a maximum capacity of 432 Imp gallons, was stored in four self-sealing wing tanks which were accessed through detachable panels forming part of the lower wing surfaces.

The interior of the Hornet was drilled from wooden templates for the ferrules which were used to attach the various items of equipment. Below left: the drill template in position. Below right: the ferrules after assembly.

To aid the pilot's field of view the unpressurised cockpit was mounted well forward in the fuselage and was housed under an aft sliding, perspex blister canopy. The three-panel windscreen was designed so that refraction through the panels meant that there were no obvious blind spots caused by the corner tie-rods; all three panels were bullet-proof laminated glass. An armour-plated bulkhead - hinged near the top to provide access to the back of the instrument panel and the rudder pedals - was part of the nose structure, with the pilot's back and head being protected by another armoured bulkhead built into the cockpit. Below and behind the cockpit floor was a bay housing the built-in armament of four short-barrelled 20 mm Hispano V cannon, firing through short blast tubes.

Top: Installing the equipment at the electical circuits stage of half-shell assembly.

Centre and right: Fore and after views of the Hornet fuselage on the boxing up fixture.

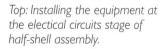

128